P9-DCY-926

PRAISE FOR *SANE NEW WORLD*

"The United States has for too long been deprived of one of our greatest comic talents—the inimitable Ruby Wax. In this book, she puts her hilarity in service of the important message that we can change our own minds to live better lives. Her disquisition will be wonderfully helpful to those whose minds need changing, and wonderfully entertaining to everyone else."

—Andrew Solomon, author of *Far from the Tree*

"Ruby Wax offers a fresh and revealing insider's view of how the potential torments of everyday life can be eased as we train our minds to enable our feelings, thoughts, and behaviors to become more stable and adaptive. As a spokesperson for the power of mindful awareness, our humorous and forthright guide offers up a unique blend of personal experience and academic education to inspire us to enhance the health of our bodies, our minds, and our relationships."

—Daniel J. Siegel, M.D., *New York Times*
bestselling author of *Brainstorm*

"Ruby Wax is brave, generous, and hilarious—the perfect guide on a tour of the brain and how its workings affect our overall well-being. And she is passionate about our collective need to tap into the power of mindfulness to help still our minds in an age of speed, hyperconnectivity, and distraction."

—Arianna Huffington, *New York Times* bestselling author of *Thrive*

"Ruby Wax is at her best in this wonderful book. Its acute observations are both extremely funny and deeply moving. Many people will be grateful for her courage, openness, humor, and wisdom."

—Mark Williams, author of *Mindfulness*

continued . . .

"Finally—a map for the troubled human mind. And it's *funny*."
　　　　　　　　—Caitlin Moran, author of *How to Be a Woman*

"Through humor and unbridled truth, Ruby Wax shares her journey to mindfulness, illuminating how it can improve our state of mind and change our brain for a healthier, happier life."
　　　　　　　　—Goldie Hawn, *New York Times* bestselling author of
　　　　　　　　10 Mindful Minutes

"Ruby Wax has an extraordinary mind, and she has brought it to bear with trademark wit and searing honesty on the subject of that mind and the minds of all of us. Very few will be able to read this wonderful contribution to the literature of mental health without recognizing some part of themselves and certainly of someone they know. A ruby beyond price."　　　　　　　　—Stephen Fry

"I love this book more than I love Ruby. And that's saying quite a bit . . . in a loud, funny voice. Yes . . . I love this book. And I know books. And I know love. And Ruby's book is both."
　　　　　　　　—Carrie Fisher

"A very funny book about how to be calm and poised and not bonkers."　　　　—Helen Fielding, author of *Bridget Jones's Diary*

"Wonderful, painfully funny, and instructive."
　　　　　　　　—Allison Pearson, author of *I Don't Know How She Does It*

"I was both amused and educated by Ruby Wax's self-help look at our brains, and the ways they're out to get us, and what we can do about it. She's a smart and funny writer on a mission to help us help ourselves. I was impressed."　　　　　　　—Neil Gaiman

"Witty, wise, and thought-provoking."　　　　　—Nigella Lawson

RUBY WAX

SANE
NEW
WORLD

A User's Guide to the
Normal-Crazy Mind

A PERIGEE BOOK

A PERIGEE BOOK
Published by the Penguin Group
Penguin Group (USA) LLC
375 Hudson Street, New York, New York 10014

USA • Canada • UK • Ireland • Australia • New Zealand • India • South Africa • China

penguin.com

A Penguin Random House Company

Copyright © 2013 by Ruby Wax
Penguin supports copyright. Copyright fuels creativity, encourages diverse voices,
promotes free speech, and creates a vibrant culture. Thank you for buying an authorized edition of
this book and for complying with copyright laws by not reproducing, scanning,
or distributing any part of it in any form without permission. You are supporting
writers and allowing Penguin to continue to publish books for every reader.

PERIGEE is a registered trademark of Penguin Group (USA) LLC.
The "P" design is a trademark belonging to Penguin Group (USA) LLC.

Library of Congress Cataloging-in-Publication Data

Wax, Ruby, date.
Sane new world : a user's guide to the normal-crazy mind / Ruby Wax.
p.   cm.
ISBN 978-0-399-17060-7
1. Mind and body.   2. Mindfulness-based cognitive therapy.   1. Title.
    BF161   W24   2014   2014016530
'   158.1—dc23

First American edition: November 2014
Originally published in Great Britain by Hodder & Stoughton in 2013.

PRINTED IN THE UNITED STATES OF AMERICA

10   9   8   7   6   5   4   3   2   1

Text design by Ellen Cipriano
Illustrations by Serge Seidlitz

"Autobiography in Five Short Chapters" from *There's a Hole in My Sidewalk: The Romance of
Self-Discovery* by Portia Nelson. Reprinted with the permission of Beyond Words/Atria Publishing
Group. Copyright © 1993 by Portia Nelson. All rights reserved.

"The Guest House" by Jalal al-Din Rumi translated by Coleman Barks with John Moyne from *The
Essential Rumi* 2004, reprinted by permission of Coleman Barks.

Illustrations by Serge Seidlitz reprinted by permission of Début Art Ltd, London.

Neither the publisher nor the author is engaged in rendering professional advice or services to the
individual reader. The ideas, procedures, and suggestions contained in this book are not intended
as a substitute for consulting with your physician. All matters regarding your health require
medical supervision. Neither the author nor the publisher shall be liable or responsible for any
loss or damage allegedly arising from any information or suggestion in this book

While the author has made every effort to provide accurate telephone numbers, Internet
addresses, and other contact information at the time of publication, neither the publisher
nor the author assumes any responsibility for errors, or for changes that occur after
publication. Further, the publisher does not have any control over and does not
assume any responsibility for author or third-party websites or their content.

Most Perigee books are available at special quantity discounts for bulk
purchases for sales promotions, premiums, fund-raising, or educational
use. Special books, or book excerpts, can also be created to fit specific
needs. For details, write: Special.Markets@us.penguingroup.com.

To Ed, Max, Marina, and Maddy

CONTENTS

THE BEGINNING

This book is dedicated to my mind, which at one point left town, and to the rest of humanity, who perhaps at one time or another might have misplaced theirs. Though I personally have gone on a roller-coaster ride of depression for most of my adult life, this book is not exclusively for the depressed. I am one of the one in four who has mentally unraveled; this book is for the four in four. It's for everyone, because we all share the same equipment: We suffer, we laugh, we rage, we bitch, we're all vulnerable, delicate creatures under our tough fronts.

In this book I am going to attempt to give a rough guide for where we (the human race) are right now and offer some suggestions that might make our time on Earth a more joyful experience. I'm not talking "everyone in the Jacuzzi" joyful, I'm talking about the almost blissful state you sometimes have when time stops, your body feels like it's home, and the volume of those internal critics in your mind lowers. I know those voices well, and so many people I meet recognize this dictator barking orders in their minds, keeping them up at night with that tormenting "I should have, I could have" tape playing relentlessly.

Many of us suffer from the pressures in today's world that drive us from burnout to depression. We are slaves to our busyness with an insatiable drive for money, fame, more tweets—you name it, we want it. The problem is, it's only in the last fifty to a hundred years that humans have lived with such abundance. We've gone from scarcity (when we were probably somewhat normal and had appetites to match) to the limitless demands we have today. You could say that multitasking has driven us mad; like leaving too many windows open on your computer, eventually it will crash. We are simply not equipped for the twenty-first century. It's too hard, too fast, it's too full of fear; we just don't have the bandwidth. Evolution did not prepare us for this. It's hard enough to keep up with who's bombing whom, so we have no room to understand our emotional landscapes; our hearts bleed because we hear of a beached whale while the next minute we're baying for the blood of someone who stole the last shopping cart.

The reason I decided to devote myself to this inward journey is because I wanted to find some shelter from the constant hurricanes of depression, which left me depleted and broken. Each episode got longer and deeper. I don't want to blame my parents but child rearing was not their specialty. Friends would come over and there my mother would be, perched on the lampshade, a vulture with a Viennese accent, waiting for someone to drop a crumb. When they did, she would swoop across the room screaming, "Who brings cookies into a building?" Everyone would run away terrified. It got much, much darker later, but I am not going to talk about that here. My point is that this is the type of background that usually leads to a career as a comedian or a serial killer; I went for the comedy.

Here's my life story so far:

Ruby Wax was born many, many years ago. She won't be exact—anywhere from thirty-five to seventy-eight years ago.

Her first word was *gargle*. Everyone had great hopes.

Her first ambition was to be a mermaid, and when that didn't work out she decided to be a squirrel. She did this for three years using an old Davy Crockett hat sewn to the back of her pants as a tail. Her dream ended when the tail blew out the window of the car her parents were driving, and they wouldn't stop for her to collect it. This damaged her, but didn't stop her.

She then went on to summer camp (Camp Agawak) where she got a special mention in canoeing.

Jump cut.

Many years later, after a calamity called her education, she went to the UK to get away from her parents. (For reasons, see her other book, *How Do You Want Me?*).

Once in the UK, she got into a drama school and after three years of practicing tongue exercises (to get the English accent she has today) she was accepted into the Royal Shakespeare Company, mainly because they liked what she could do with her tongue.

She began her five years there performing small parts that included:

Whore/Nun (*Measure for Measure*)
Nonspeaking Spirit (*The Tempest*)
Waitress with no lines (*Antony and Cleopatra*)
And many others

She got sick of having no lines so she began to write her own shows in which she played the lead and had the other members of the company play her maidservants and ashtrays.

From that point on, a fellow thespian at the RSC, Alan Rickman, directed and helped mold her career as clearly she was not going to be a successful classical actress. He has said many times he would never work with her again.

She then leaped to fame working in television for the next twenty-five years on her own comedy documentaries and in comedy and interview shows.

She wrote and performed in *Girls on Top* with Dawn French and Jennifer Saunders and Tracey Ullman, which was very popular with gay people, and so she was launched.

Ruby script edited every season of *Absolutely Fabulous* and also performed in it, the likes of "Menopause Woman" just as an example.

Her own television shows included *Wax on Wheels, Don't Miss*

Wax, Wax in America, Wax Acts, Wax On . . . All these shows were basically about Ruby and her guests: Jim Carrey, Tom Hanks, O.J. Simpson (who tried to knife her with a banana—look on YouTube), Imelda Marcos (who showed Ruby her new stash of shoes and even gave her some), and too many others to name.

She has recently received her master's degree from Oxford University, graduating in mindfulness-based cognitive therapy in September 2013.

Ruby used her research for her dissertation at Oxford to write this book (with a comedy spin), along with her new one-woman show with the same title and her speech for TED Talk Global called "What's So Funny About Mental Illness?" Thereby killing three birds with one gun.

BACK TO THIS BOOK

So, after some serious breakdowns, I decided to go back to school to study psychotherapy to figure out exactly what they were charging £80 an hour for. I used to leave my shrink knowing exactly who I was, until I got to the tube station and then I'd forget again. Also, as I knew nothing about psychology; therapists could tell me anything, so how could I tell if they were any good? Once, when I was on the couch, I caught the shrink behind me eating a pastrami sandwich, mustard all over his face.

So I went to study psychotherapy. I got a library card and never discussed my previous life again. I thought, "Let's give something back to the world." (I probably didn't but it's a good line.) I've noticed that many women like myself choose to study therapy when they meet the wild surf of menopause; the hormones dry up, and they realize the chances are low they're ever going to be hit on again, so they find themselves wanting to care for other people or starting a rest home for stray cats.

A few years later, I decided to go further and learn about what I was really interested in: the brain. My thinking was, if I learned how my own engine worked, it might prevent me from getting stuck in the middle of nowhere, shrieking for someone to come and fix me; I would provide my own AAA service. I'd be able to lasso this wild beast of a brain, stop it from churning away over the same ground, keeping me up at nights; worrying, rehashing, regretting, and resenting.

After much research, I thought mindfulness might help me best as I had heard it gives you the ability to regulate your own mind. (I would say it saved my life, but I'll get to that later in the book.) I decided to go straight to the horse's mouth, to one of the founders of mindfulness-based cognitive therapy, Professor Mark Williams, who told me that unfortunately I would have to get into Oxford University in order to study it alongside neuroscience.

I scraped together some old school records and managed to excavate my one or two decent high school grades, but most of all I give great interview, so I got into that master's course. The other fourteen students in my class were very brilliant and looked at me on day one as if they were having an encounter of the third kind; but God dammit, I was there.

So after many decades of agonizing investigation, a master's in mindfulness, a degree in psychotherapy, and even a small taste of fame, here I am writing this manual on how to tame your mind.

I'll go into detail later but I want to mention one fact right away; the gold at the end of the rainbow is that *you can change your mind and how you think*. This is called neuroplasticity. Your genes, hormones, regions in the brain, and early learning do not necessarily determine your fate.

Scientific evidence has shown that neurons (brain cells) can rewire and change patterns throughout your lifetime as a result of your experiences and how you think about them. So your thoughts affect the physiology of your brain and the physiology affects your thoughts.

> *You can change your mind and how you think.*

Think about sex for a minute. That's OK, I'll wait. Once you get an inkling, a whole cascade of hormones is let loose in your body to get you ready to cha-cha. Sometimes it's the other way around; you're minding your own business, and for no reason a hormone switches on in your brain and suddenly your thinking goes X-rated.

When your mind changes, your brain changes—and because our brains are so malleable, the sky's the limit. I remind you that I got into Oxford in my fifties even though I failed to get a diploma from Busy Beaver nursery school (look it up, that was the actual name), proving really anything is possible. But it takes time to alter your habits of thinking; it won't happen with a weekend workshop called "How to Tickle Your Inner Angel." It takes intentional concentration and repetition over time. You can change but only if you make the effort not to do the same old thing, the same old way, day in and day out. You, and the way you see the world, are the architect of how your brain is mapped. This is what scientists are giving us in the twenty-first century; way beyond what Psychic Madge can read in your palm.

The brain is like a pliable three-pound piece of Play-Doh; you can resculpt it by breaking old mental habits and creating new, more flexible ways of thinking. Gloria Gaynor was wrong when she sang, "I am what I am." She will have to change those lyrics, but it won't be so easy to dance to. What rhymes with neuroplasticity?

THE INNER YOU

If you could look inside your brain and roughly understand where everything is and how it operates, you might not be able to completely know yourself, but with practice you may be able to fix yourself. Learning how to self-regulate means you can sense the early warnings before a full-on burnout or depression and do something about it. So much is known about this idea of self-regulation; it may (and I hope it does) shortly become the buzzword of the decade. We can, with certain practices such as mindfulness, actually have some control over the chemicals in our brains that drive us to stress, to anxiety, and even to happiness. This remarkable organ in our heads holds infinite wisdom but so few of us know how to use it. It's similar to having a Ferrari but no one gave you the keys.

The reality is that the demanding voice in our heads is not who we are. It plays a very small part in the big scheme of things. What's really running you is a million, trillion gigabyte–powered engine room in your brain, managed by your DNA, that instructs hormones, memories, muscles, blood, organs, and really everything that happens inside you to ensure that you survive at all costs, and not that stupid inner monologue about why you're too fat to wear tights.

My aim in this book is to show you how to become the master of your mind and not the slave. If you learn how to self-regulate your moods, emotions, and thoughts and focus your mind on what you want to pay attention to rather than be dragged into distraction, you might just reach that elusive thing called happiness. We all have it; we just don't know where the on button is. The organ that allows you to realize the world understands so little about itself.

(Yes, Oprah, I'm available.)

WHY WE NEED A MANUAL

What is our purpose on Earth? Everyone wants to know. So the question is not, To be or not to be? The big questions are, What are we meant to be doing while we're being? and, How do I run and manage this thing called me? Our primary problem as a species (I leave out those with religious beliefs—they have their own books) is that we have no manual, no instructions that tell us how to live our lives. Domestic appliances have instruction manuals; not us. We're born with absolutely no information and are reliant on Mommy and Daddy who jam their USB sticks into our innocent hard drives and download their neuroses into us. As I think we've agreed, we're all missing a manual, so I've tried to keep it simple.

Part 1: What's Wrong with Us? For the Normal-Mad

In Part 1 of this book I examine why we are all in the flying-by-the-seat-of-our-pants school of thought when it comes to living our lives. We assume the next person knows what they're doing; they don't.

Part 2: What's Wrong with Us? For the Mad-Mad

Part 2 is for the depressed, anxious, panic-attacked, OCD'd, overeaters, drinkers, shoppers, compulsive list-makers, and so on. The roll call is endless.

Part 3: What's in Your Brain/What's on Your Mind?

In Part 3 I familiarize you with your ingredients: the hormones, neurons, hemispheres, regions, and so on, so that in Part 4 you'll be able to understand what physically happens in your brain when you practice mindfulness and how it can enhance positive feelings, which ultimately bring happiness.

You are your own cookbook. How you work your brain determines if you're going to become filet mignon or an old soggy meatball.

Part 4: Mindfulness: Taming Your Mind

Think of Part 4 as "Wisdom for Dummies." I'll show you how to be able to self-regulate your thoughts and emotions to make you the *master* and not the *slave* of your mind.

Part 5: Alternative Suggestions for Peace of Mind

I would never want to be considered evangelical, so if mindfulness isn't for you, in Part 5 I give you alternative practices that can help change your brain.

I hope this book helps you let go of the image you have of yourself if it's getting in your way; I hope I can encourage you to be brave and know that nothing is certain: life flows, changes, and ends. Get over your fear. The only way to find any peace is to let it all go and jump into the unknown. Just jump.

PART ONE

WHAT'S WRONG WITH US? FOR THE NORMAL-MAD

WHAT DRIVES
US CRAZY

There may be many observations in this part that do not resonate with you, but we see the world only through our own eyes. I know there are people out there who don't see the world as I do, but sadly they aren't writing this book. So if anyone does not suffer from what follows, I apologize if it seems I'm painting the whole human race with the same pessimistic brush. I have reached these conclusions only because everyone I have ever met has complained that these are the areas of life that drive them crazy. I know from the bottom of my heart, they are what drive me crazy.

CRITICAL VOICES

Why are we so mean to ourselves? What did we do wrong? Why, if we are the best that evolution has tossed up so far, are we so abusive to ourselves? Each of us has a nagging parent implanted in our heads: "Don't do that . . . why didn't you . . . you should have . . . but you didn't," on an endless tape. (My mother would say she was telling me what a failure I was only because she loved me.) If most of us ever compared our inner leitmotif, we would sue each other for plagiarism, as our internal themes are so alike.

No other species is as cruel as we are to ourselves. We'd never dream of treating our pets the way we treat ourselves. We whip ourselves to keep moving like we would an old horse, until it falls over exhausted; the hooves made into glue. I have asked so many people if they have ever had a voice in their head that says, "Congratulations you've done a wonderful job and may I say how attractive you look today." The answer is no one. I'm sure they're out there I just never met them.

Once you get an attack of this self-immolation, you're on the slippery slope to a very unhappy state. Your brain just churns away, chewing over a problem like a piece of meat that won't go down. There will never be a solution to "I should have," so you attack, guess who? You. This is why one in four of us is mentally ill.

It's not our fault that we're slave drivers to ourselves because biologically we all have this factory-installed chip that compels us to achieve and move forward. Before we even had words, we had an innate drive in every cell of our body to press on at all costs. (Google "selfish gene.") This is how one cell becomes two, and two becomes three (I could go on but I haven't got time).

Cells keep advancing to the trillion cells that finally make up us and when language came on-line a mere 75,000 or so years ago we started to translate that compulsion to improve with that inner monologue of "I should have," "I could have," "I'm going to screw up." That old familiar tune.

Each of us internalizes the voices in our heads from our parents, who probably meant well, but these sentiments stay in there for a lifetime. It's because most parents want to protect their children that you get an abundance of "you shouldn't have . . . you should have," otherwise the child might put their finger in a light socket and blow up. These corrective voices helped you survive as a child; later in life they can either drive you mad with their constant corrections and instructions or they can help you successfully navigate obstacles throughout your life, giving you a smoother ride.

There are parents who encourage their children with positive reinforcement and calming encouragement: "That's right sweetheart, you did so well, why don't we try it again and you'll be even better?" These children, later in life, may see a close friend passing by who doesn't acknowledge them, and their inner voice says, "Oh, too bad, Fiona must be preoccupied and she looks so lovely, I'll call her later." Those of us with parents trained by the Attila the Hun school of child rearing would react to this incident with, "Fiona hates my guts, that's why she's ignoring me. She found out I'm a moron, which I am."

MY STORY

In my case, I would say the voices were somewhat harsh for a baby; they were less like suggestions and more like commando orders. My mother had a fear of dust so she'd have a sponge in each hand and two stuck to her knees (my mother was completely absorbent) and she'd crawl around behind me on all fours screaming, "Who puts footprints on a carpet? Are they criminally insane?" She probably wanted to protect me, from what I don't know, but I was hermetically sealed in my house as a child; everything was wrapped in plastic, including my father, my grandmother, and the dog. Both my parents had to escape Nazi Austria in a laundry basket, just before "last orders" was shouted and the borders shut down so no one could leave the Fatherland. This probably is what made her so fearful, which she unconsciously projected onto dust balls. (They're easier to blow away.) Whatever the case, I picked up the panic in her voice, and that sound has never left my head. So even though I'm not in Nazi Austria, the voices in my head are. Not anyone's fault.

THE SEARCH FOR HAPPINESS

We are all looking for happiness (unless of course we've already got it, and blessed are those few who have). This is why we have so many self-help books—enough now to cover the equator seventy-eight times. Have you read *The Secret*? I didn't read it but I know eighty million copies were sold. I did read page one, which informs you that "the secret" was handed down to us by the ancient Babylonians and clearly it worked for them; that's why there's so many running around, you can't move for all the Babylonians living in London. Next, the author tells you that Plato, Leonardo da Vinci, Beethoven, and Einstein were inspired by this book. I'm going to use that idea and give myself reviews from dead people. Apparently the next two hundred pages are filled with advice that boils down to, "Think happy thoughts and your dreams will come true, just like Tinker Bell promised." (I'm sorry to all you fans of *The Secret*, I'm just very bitter about the eighty million copies sold. You can understand.)

All of this self-help was stolen from Walt Disney; he was the father of the New Age. "Whistle a happy tune; if you believe in fairies, clap your hands." From this philosophy flowed *The Little Mermaid*, *Snow White*, and some early Mickey Mouse. Walt knew the secret of happiness. Too bad he's on ice; we've got to defrost this guy to squeeze out some more wisdom. Walt knew when to make an exit.

STAYING BUSY

Busyness is a method we have devised in order to distract ourselves from the bigger, deeper questions; we have an obsession to keep busy. There is no time to rest and no time to think about what we really should be doing in our limited time on Earth. I'm not criticizing; I'm as driven as the next person. It almost got to the point where I went into labor while doing a TV show. The floor manager gave me "Five-four-three-two," someone cut the cord and yelled, "Action."

Gandhi said, "There is more to life than speed." Unfortunately he didn't tell us what, he just left us hanging while he pranced around in his diaper.

To compensate for this undercurrent of uselessness, we pretend we're all terribly important and that we have something to bring to the world. That's why we have Twitter—so we can check how many followers we've got. We can count them; a hundred or a thousand people you've never met, telling you what they had for lunch, now knowing you exist. That's how we see if we matter. We're like little birds, newly hatched from our eggs going, "Tweet, tweet, tweet," looking for a little attention, a little love, maybe even a worm—anything will do as long as they notice we're here.

In reality we're all as disposable as wax figures. Once you lose your job or beauty or status, which you will eventually, they melt you down and use you to make the next important person. I went to Madame Tussauds and there was Charlie Chaplin next to the loo while Nicole Kidman was melted down and made into 150 candles; an icon one minute, a candle the next. Jerry Hall must be on a birthday cake somewhere.

We run because we don't want to look inside and see that there might not be anything there and that our search for meaning is a waste of airtime. We stay busy so we don't have to think about how futile the running is; like dung beetles building a house made of manure, we don't stop and think, "Hey, where's this going?"

When I have a day off and wake up, I jolt up from the pillow, panicking that I may have nothing of any importance to do. Maybe this is why I, and people I know like me, have to keep busy compiling an endless to-do list. For us, busyness is our god. We worship it. People ask me if I'm busy and I tell them, "I'm so busy I've had two heart attacks." They congratulate me on this achievement.

We hold those who are on the tightest of schedules in reverence; the busier you are, the higher your status as a human being. For those of us who suffer from this phenomenon, we have sped up to such a frenzy of things "to do," we make ourselves ill just to avoid having to look inside and see that we might not have any point at all. So who is ultimately the winner? The busy, running people? Or maybe it's someone who sits on a rock and fishes all day or someone who has the time to feel the breeze on his face? Who is the real winner? (Please dear God, I hope it's not the guy with the fish.)

Here are some common answers to the question "Are you busy?"

"I am run off my feet."
   (Let's picture it, someone somewhere was dashing
      at such a rate that he or she literally cracked at
      the ankle and just kept going.)

"I don't know if I'm coming or going."
>   (Someone once opened a door and just stayed there
>   for the next five years trying to figure, "In or
>   out?")

If you have used either of these responses, then you probably are an A-list person who is living the life, even though you are too busy to have one.

There are women in my neighborhood in London who have nothing to do for a living and they are booked to the hilt. They do Pilates five times a week so they can make their pelvic floor strong enough to lift the carpet. Dyson could use them as vacuums. Then they'll shop with their personal shopper (that takes up a few hours), have their hair blow-dried (that's another hour), lunch (that's a four-hour filler). Then they have to pick up the kids and do their homework for them, and then it's time to get ready and go off to attend a charity event. You know what that entails? They go to a really fancy hotel and pay $2,000 a plate to save a tuna.

NEVER ENOUGH

These Pilates women complain that their husbands work until midnight and they're left having to get their spawn into a nursery school that only takes kids whose IQs have six digits. I have (in vain) tried to tell them that marriage is a "negotiated deal."

I've even made them a little flow-chart so they can get some perspective. I tell them, "If your husband is earning more than $150,000 a year, plus bonuses, you as the wife have no rights. You take care of the house and the kids. You must give him sex whenever and wherever he wants. And you have to stay thin and young till death do you part.

"If your husband is making around $75,000 a year, you still take care of the house and kids but you may bitch about him up to twenty-seven hours a week to your friends. If he does not help on the weekends, you can withhold the sex.

"If he makes below $20,000 a year, you can let the house and kids go to hell." That's all for when the husband is making all the money.

If the wife is making all the money, say, she's earning $150,000 a year, which is equivalent to $575,000 in "Man Money," she will still have to do everything because evolution has not given men eyes to see details such as a hoofprint on the carpet. But man does have a very important function, and that is to stand there and gaze toward the horizon to make sure there are no wildebeests.

Shopping Is Our Search for Love

This need to have more is not limited to the wives of football players or head honchos of big organizations. We all, in our own way, never stop wanting, that's why we need twenty thousand feet of mall; big steaming mounds of galleria won't be enough to satisfy. The shopping never stops; the label says it all.

Our self-esteem drives us to buy a designer handbag that costs the GNP of Croatia, which is why people with nothing will spend their last shekel on Dolce & Gabbana or a $300 pair of Nikes. If you have the tattoo of CC on your handbag, you can get a nod of respect from everyone who passes, even though you're homeless. I once saw a tramp in Miami pushing all his belongings in a shopping cart he stole from Bloomingdale's. He was wearing newspaper and had a cap on his head that read, "Born to Shop."

What we throw on our back is our new means of identity. People who wear Prada usually hang out with other Praderites and the same with all other brands; people seek their own level, their own tribe. Picture it, a whole gaggle of Guccis at the watering hole or outlet mall, as we call it today, eating a carcass.

P.S. Proof of our insanity is that we actually buy UGG boots. Where in the brain do we feel a need to look like an Eskimo, as if they had any fashion sense? They may counter that they wear them for warmth but it still looks like they're walking in a beaver.

THE FIX OF HAPPINESS

Some people think to reach a state of joy, you need to dress in sheets for a lifetime, have a dot on your head, and sit on top of a mountain. Some wave crystals, eat turf, pray, chant, and dance with the wolves. Contentment might even be possible. . . . I'm sure it's feasible to sit on a bench and feed a squirrel without getting antsy. But the trouble is, we always want more. We're the A-list of all species so we go for the Golden Chalice: happiness. It had to be a crazy American who said that we all have the right to pursue happiness. That's why you hear them demanding a double latte caramel macchiato every morning with their smiling teeth just before they chirp, "Have a nice day." There are some lucky people who feel they experience happiness when they gaze at a cloud or walk on the beach, but the rest of us get that special tingly buzz only when we've bought, won, achieved, hooked, or booked something. Then our own brains give us a hit of dopamine, which makes us feel good. We don't need substances; we are our own drug dealers.

The problem is, the hit of happiness usually lasts as long as a cigarette, so we have to continually search for the next fix. It's as though as a species we had no brakes, only breakdowns. Mother Nature's little joke on us is that the original object of desire isn't so much fun when we get it, so unless we can up the stakes all the time, we can't get that burst of internal fireworks we call happiness. Most animals just eat their fill and walk away, but not us—we keep glutting ourselves even though the next bite never tastes as good as the first one.

The Hierarchy of Western Wants (According to Me)

- Food and/or water
- Mattress
- Roof
- House

- Normal car
- Second house
- Pool
- Porsche
- Flying economy class
- Business class
- First class
- Private jet
- Private jet with jacuzzi
- Meeting Oprah

This failure to get what we want leaves us in a state of permanent desire. Magazines understand that they make us salivate for the unobtainable; the chase is better than the kill. People who collect art pay $20 million for some semen on a cracker and then never notice it once it's on their wall. They'll be back licking the pages of Sotheby's catalog for what they crave next. If we're not wanting, we're waiting. Waiting for what, we don't know, but something and it's going to happen soon. Waiting for our screenplay to be commissioned about a clown who falls in love with a squirrel and then decides to become a car dealer. Waiting for the money to roll in for an idea about inventing soup in a solid form; it's all about to happen next week, next year, we don't mind how long, as long as we're in a suspended state of waiting.

A new phenomenon that arises from our insatiable appetites is the sense of entitlement that is the disease of this age; now everyone thinks they deserve to be a winner. This is why so many deluded people with absolutely no sense of shame have the audacity to try out for *X Factor* when they have the voice of a toad. Self-help books will tell you that the only thing standing in your way is you.

"You can be beautiful if you think you are," they say. This is why you see the truly self-deluded paint their nails with tiny diamantes embedded in bloodbath-red extensions, as if no one will notice that they are the size of Tibet. Or you get Sarah Palin thinking she can run a country.

NEGATIVE THINKING

Once we humans have the basics for survival—that is, food, water, and mascara—you would think we should be on our knees, kissing the ground in gratitude for our aliveness, for being able to see through our eyes, hear through our ears, and best of all, eat. Let us have a moment's silence to thank the Big Bang for making it possible that eventually we could experience the taste of Ben & Jerry's Chunky Monkey. But even with all these miracles we still suffer, and it's all because of our negative thinking. Animals don't have negative thoughts; they're out there having the time of their lives, swinging from branches, mating with nearly everyone who comes up behind them. And us? We ruminate on things, worry, regret, resent. Who picked the short straw, do you think? Most awful of all is that we can project to the future and figure out that we will eventually lose our looks and dare I say it . . . die.

See how there's always a grenade at the bottom of the cookie jar? It's so like the story of my life—whenever I achieve a little something and am complimented, shortly thereafter I am swiftly kicked in the ass by karma. The more you have (looks, money, fame) the more you suffer when you lose it. There is always a bill to pay. Luckily, they bless a few people with a dollop of unawareness so when they begin to crinkle and melt into oblivion, they're the last to know and they just keep on kickin' those "hoofers" on ole Broadway, even though you hear the sound of their arthritic hips cracking in the effort. (This probably sounds judgmental, but I get evolved later in the book so just bear with me now.)

Those of us who aren't on the brink of starvation or elimination or living in squalor are condemned to a life of worrying about trivia. It all went downhill when we crawled out of the jungle. We just don't know what to think about next after fulfilling basic needs; so we make over our kitchens. In my neighborhood all the surfaces in this year's kitchens are buffed silver metal resembling what you'd find in mortuaries. You're scared to open a drawer in case a toe hangs out with a label dangling from it. Now they are digging down below the kitchens to make more floors until they hit volcanic rock. Some have lap pools they will never lap in. I know someone who is building an underground vineyard.

BATHROOMS OF GRANDEUR

I have a theory that you can tell how mentally deranged someone is by viewing their bathroom. If they believe they need a
chandelier, an Italian marble tub, and a toilet that performs more
than three functions (now some of them play Rachmaninoff
when you lift the lid and squirt you with lilac perfume after you
pee) they are not a well person and have strayed far, far away
from sanity. Freud should have come up with a therapy where
you interrogate the clients about how they envision the decor
of their bathrooms rather than asking about sex. Sex tells you
nothing. How you want your lavatory to look is the gateway to
the unconscious. A bathroom is a place where there is no room
in there for narcissism. It's where you really see yourself for
what you are and get a whiff of reality. On the toilet no one is
a star. Remember that and you will go far in life.

OUR NEED TO BE SPECIAL

Our status used to be based on bloodlines—on whether you
were a Princess or a Pea. Now we determine each other's worth
by asking, "What do you do?" If you say, "I do nothing," people move away from you as if you are a corpse. Our identity is
on our business cards, and new titles emerge every year to define increasingly abstract roles. Job descriptions like "consultant" and "thought leader" are ambiguous at best. (If everyone's

a consultant, who is left needing one?) These days motivational speakers are also considered big shots. We confuse bravery with bravado. I've seen motivational speakers who are brought in to companies to tell you about rowing across the Atlantic with one arm. How is this helping the company? That person isn't brave, he's nuts. And these speakers are starting to get competitive; apparently someone has claimed he climbed Mount Everest using only his nostrils.

Each of us thinks somewhere inside we have a purpose. Long ago we didn't have this existentialist angst; we were hunters or gatherers. A hunter hunted, a gatherer gathered (Jewish people pointed instead of doing either). Back then there was no such thing as individuality so you couldn't distinguish "you" from anyone else unless you wore a hat or had more hair but basically we were all the same: grunting and foraging.

In those days you didn't need a manual. You were born, drove an ox around a field, multiplied, and died. No one complained; plagues came and went—smallpox, influenza, you name them, you had them—and everyone had the same attitude: "Shit happens." Now it's an outrage: "How dare some virus wipe us out? Does it know who we are? We're superior beings, the crème de la crème of all that live and breathe; top of the food chain."

It all went wrong when some deluded optimist wrote the words, "All men are created equal." This is clearly not the case; some people are losers. He never even lived to see the can of worms he released once he wrote that with his feather. He just signed his autograph and let the chaos begin. (I'm going to name names. It was Thomas Jefferson—another American.)

THE BIG TEAM: HAPPY DAYS

We were at our happiest when we used to drive our yoke-necklaced oxen around a field because then we were all working together as a big tribe, a team. OK, it was tough, but we had some laughs out there in the blizzard conditions (without UGGs). We needed to form tribes in order to fight off neighboring tribes who tried to steal our oxen. Without an ox you were nothing. After that, the number of people in a tribe diminished because along came the gun and then you didn't really need a lot of people, just one guy with a good trigger finger. That's why now we don't have this sense of teamwork; we're all alone hunkering in our corners, clutching our weapons.

The only time we do get a sense of belonging to a tribe is when we're facing a disaster like a hurricane, Godzilla, or a war. In the UK the only time everyone unites is when they're reminiscing about World War II; when they get fueled up on the Blitzkrieg spirit, they all start blubbering away singing those "We'll Meet Again" songs they heard on the wireless. Every Christmas, my husband's parents would dress up as Luftwaffe and RAF pilots and run around the living room going, "We shall fight them on the beaches!" and screaming, "We shall never surrender," as they smashed into the TV set.

In my opinion, our downfall began when we started to

think of ourselves as "individuals." I read somewhere—don't ask me where—that hundreds and hundreds of years ago there was no word for *I*. There was only the word for *we*. No one was lonely back then. The trouble started when the individual came into the picture. Remember the wheel? Back millions of years ago when we made the wheel? We don't know who made it. There was no wheel by Chanel. Remember when we all worked together to make fire? We don't know who lit the first match—he was just some guy and he didn't need his name in lights. Now agents and managers have to get involved and skim 20 percent off the top for just standing there.

Simple animals have all the luck. They're delighted to still work as a team. They're delighted to be part of a gaggle, or flock, or swarm. Goose in the back row of the flying formation? He's proud to be there. He's overjoyed. It's his job in life. Not us anymore. Our earliest instinct is to bond together and socialize; our very DNA gives us instructions on how to mingle.

You know whom I blame for all this? Freud. If he hadn't mentioned an ego, we would never have had one. Because of him it's all about me. Me, I need to be the next Kate Moss. Me, I need to run Apple. Me, I need to be in *People*, and I'll do anything to get on television. "You want me to eat my mother-in-law? Toss her on the barbecue."

So this is the human condition: We're living longer, getting taller, and are a push of a finger away from every other person on the planet and yet we do not know how to run ourselves.

Maybe we're not supposed to know, and when we're finished filling the world with parking lots, artisanal muffin shops, and Starbucks, our point on Earth is finished and with one big cataclysmic boom we'll be gone.

Millions of years of natural selection, and this is what we've come to. We want to be the most famous, the richest, the thinnest and the busiest. Darwin would shit in his pants.

THE PROBLEM WITH CHANGE

I have given you a preview of the good news already: *We can change.* But here I ought to point out, as we are focusing on the problems of living in modern times, that when you do change, those around you won't like it. People will not easily let go of their image of you, even though you have thoroughly redecorated your inner self. They want you to stay as they remember you so that they feel they aren't changing either, that they are still gloriously youthful. This is why we don't want to see an aging movie star because it makes us think of our own mortality. Sometimes they will cast an "older" woman (in her fifties!) but they'll make sure she dies of something terminal halfway through. No one wants to see an aging face on the screen, especially in HD. (I once saw myself in HD; I looked like a close-up of an elephant.) We run to doctors to fight off Mr. Gravity for another year but it's hopeless. We should tell ourselves, "The Christmas tree is dead already, stop trying to decorate it with shiny tinsel, it won't help."

I'm not leaving myself out of this; I give thanks every day to surgeons who have helped me look this pert long after pertness should have died. I'm sure my insides are like the old Dorian Gray, while my face looks all shiny and new. I once said to Jennifer Saunders wasn't it amazing that you couldn't tell I've had any work done on my face? She said that I was delusional and that it was obvious. I will never tell anyone how old I am. The year I was born will never pass these lips without cruel and unusual punishment first. Actually, I don't even remember the year I was born. I set my burglar alarm to remind me. My house has been robbed many times, but when the police come over I can't remember what I set the alarm at: 1971? 1932? 1995? Could be anything.

We can change.

So many people want to label you as funny or aggressive or a mess. We are condemned by other people to stagnate in the image they have of us; held ransom by their expectations like a butterfly pinned on cardboard. I'm still asked by taxi drivers, as if this wouldn't hurt me, why I am no longer on television. In the past, I used to have to choke back the bile as I felt that stab in my heart. I used to answer with "Because I have terminal cancer." That usually shut them up pretty quick. I stopped doing that because I've learned that if you take out your anger on someone, it comes back to you like acid reflux, and you've poisoned yourself and feel toxic and nauseated while the taxi driver probably just goes back to his home and wife and has a lovely life.

I had to change, I didn't have a choice as my career in television was pulled out like a rug from under me and I was replaced by a younger (but not as funny) version of me. Anyway, I let it go and yes, it's painful at first when no one looks at you. Fame is very addictive and as our spotlight fades, most people are desperate to cling on and we'll do anything. "Please do a documentary about my gallbladder operation. I'll even play a corpse."

Eventually it's quite liberating to not be noticed and you rejoin the human race. When you go on the tube and no one recognizes you, it's a wakeup call; you realize how up your own ass you have been and that now it's time to come out and smell the bus and subway stations. There's a downside to becoming a normal person; when you tell the ticket guy at the exit that you forgot to buy a ticket and you think he'll go, "Ha ha you're the one from TV," and let you off, you discover that this time he doesn't and he tells you to get a ticket or you'll be arrested.

When I decided to reinvent myself (which we all have to do in life at least five times, because we were meant to be dead by thirty) and I went back to school to learn how to be a therapist, my friends said that the clients would think it was a joke. They would expect TV cameras to be following me into the room and either freak out or start auditioning. I was under the impression that the woman (me) who had that job in television was effectively dead.

The point is, we're all changing all the time. You once found it hard to tie a shoelace and now you don't even have to look. The change is so subtle; you think that whatever you feel like right now is how you always felt. Our brain can trick us into thinking that life stands still. In the end this causes the human race the most heartache.

BLINKERED VISION

As you get older you don't see many things as unique anymore. Whatever we experience in the present, we automatically go back through the Filofax in our minds to figure out what it reminds us of. We do this for the sake of survival so, say, we have had a bad experience with a man with a moustache, now we don't trust anyone with a moustache. And because we see everyone through the filter of who they remind us of, whomever we meet is therefore labeled with that image, frozen in ice for all time. We're not aware of how biased our memories make us and how they affect our view of the world.

And as we get older, our lenses get more and more narrow and blurry until we only see our own tiny pinpoint view; this limited vision eventually makes bigots of us all. This is why so many marriages fall apart. You meet someone, think that you know him, marry him, and then ten years later you divorce him because he turned out not to be who you thought he was. He never was. I realized many years after I married that I chose my husband because he has the eyebrows of Jeff Bridges. Now, I have to live daily with the disappointment that it's actually him I'm with and not Jeff. God knows who he thought I was.

It goes further. We then unconsciously create situations that back up our beliefs, just to prove our point of view is right. We all know those women who keep dating the same kind of guy just to keep up their image of themselves as victim and to reinforce the fact that all men are bastards. They give you stories about how he seemed so perfect on the "Serial Killer" website and yet, after leaving a grenade on the pillow, he never called again. Why?

It's amazing how we will suffer pain and abuse to keep our lives predictable. We'll let our inner voices brutalize us, rather than live with the possibility that we might be wrong about how we see things. We'll think, "Well at least it's a pain that's familiar."

Uncertainty is our biggest fear so we keep up the idea that our vision of the world is reality. We use our minds to construct a picture of the world, judging it, making sure it fits with our past image of things and then anticipating how our past behaviors might affect the future. We never see the world as it really is but only how we choose to see it. And because we're trapped in our own interpretation, we are prepared to go to war with other people caught in *their* view of reality—and never the twain shall meet. All this is the sound of people embedded in their own lives, believing their reality is the only reality, thinking the things they think are the only ones that matter; it's the sound of solipsism. This could be why the world is in such bad shape. It is the nub of all our problems, and until we realize how limited our views are, we'll never agree on anything. We have to try to see what other people see, through their eyes; only then can we come up with some cohesive resolution. This is my statement on world peace: take it or leave it.

MY STORY

I don't mind change. I come from a long line of unpredictability, as my ancestors didn't stick around for long in any one place. Maybe it's because I'm the daughter of immigrants that I'm always ready to jump ship, to change my location fast in case we're exterminated again. My fellow immigrants don't get sentimental about things like furniture or heirlooms; this is because we're constantly scuttling across borders, fleeing with pianos on our backs.

My fantasy is living in a simple hotel room, with no knick-knacks, only a phone for room service. I never get it when I see people waving their national flag, getting all weepy, singing some dirge about their homeland. Everyone sobbing for the old country (which is just a wet piece of peat moss) going on and on about how many generations back their people lived on this potato farm (said with an Irish accent) and how they loved it even though they've probably emigrated to another country. To me it's dirt; to them it's land—same thing. My people this, my people that. I have no real people except when I was in the mental institution and then it was full of them. They were my people, because they did not answer with "fine" when you asked how they were. We didn't need a flag.

My career ended with a bang in that I ended up in an asylum. We're always surprised when something ends; everything ends, so why do we never think it's our turn? One of my last interviews was with a famous Hollywood actor who answered my questions with only "yes" and "no," and I knew I had a car crash on my hands. Actually the very last interview show I did was with a star (who shall remain nameless) whose publicity agent allowed me only to go shopping with her in her friend's shop where she wandered around saying things like, "This is nice." Then we went to her Pilates class where I was allowed to film her doing a sit-up. She finally spoke at the end of the show in a coffee shop, and I got a forty-five-minute speech about politics in Palestine or Panama or Bosnia; it was all my fault, the whole Bush administration was my fault. I knew the show needed some comedy so on the way out of the coffee shop I bought her (only in New York) a plastic donkey into whose behind you could put a lighted cigarette and watch the smoke come out of its mouth. She held it and looked at me as if to say, "You are lower than a worm." That was the last time I interviewed anyone. As I watched them try to edit in one usable sentence I knew it was over; I would be bidding a fond farewell to this profession.

On the way down the escalator of show business, I finally hit the basement when I made a double suicide pact with Richard E. Grant by doing a show I hope you missed called Celebrity Shark Bait. Here's a clue; the sharks weren't the celebrities. We (I) did it for the money and a chance to see Cape Town, and we put the swimming with great white sharks on the back burner of our minds. Besides us on this show, there was also a girl (forgot name) from some soap (forgot name) who wore very low-cut tops to show off her white, milky breasts. They filmed her most days, and Richard and I were told they didn't need us, so we told real estate agents we were looking for a house to buy and snooped into people's homes. Meanwhile, Milky Breasts was now being filmed (I'm not making this up) in a freezer where dead pigs were hanging from hooks all around her while she stood freezing in her bikini. The point of this was to prepare her for the cold water. P.S. We were going to wear wet suits for the dive so there was no point in the pig scene except to see her nipples.

The day came for the shark dive; an instructor explained the do's and don'ts of how to behave in the shark cage. The woman, who had "Shark Lady" printed on her red jacket, told us not to worry as she had been doing this for over twenty-five years and it was perfectly safe. As she tossed large chunks of tuna into the sea for chumming (getting some blood in the water to attract the great white sharks and drive them into a feeding frenzy), we noticed she had only two fingers. It turns out Milky Breasts wouldn't get in the water—she was too scared—and so Richard and I were lowered down as bait. Suddenly something about twenty feet long glided at us, looked at us with dead eyes and swam away. The shark must have known our television careers were over and went off looking for an A-list celebrity. We became hysterical at the bottom of the cage; I laughed until urine came out of my rubber wet suit collar. Months later we *saw the show. We (I) were used as cutaways to the Breasts and when we were lowered in the cage they dubbed in screaming, thus not only humiliating us but making us look like wimps; two old has-beens sunk in the bottom of a tube. I decided to let go of show business and begin again, slowly weaning myself off fame.*

So I'm not nostalgic about leaving things. As far as my career or my university or my hometown went, I was on the bus out of town at the right time because I knew to walk away before I was pushed out. I never wanted to be the last one to leave the party. If you don't move on, you get stuck, and it becomes pathetic when you're left clutching to your past, remembering your school days, singing the old songs, and boring everyone to death. The ultimate freedom lies in knowing that everything, including you, is in a state of flux; you're never still, you're always "nexting"; billions of your cells are born, billions die. In seven years you will be a whole new version of you and the old you, a pile of dandruff flakes.

HAVE WE OVERLOADED? HOW MUCH SHOULD WE KNOW?

Our little brains are on a daily drip-feed of everything from fashion tips to traffic updates to terrorist attacks. Is there a limit? I'd like to know. I wish there were some kind of service that tells you how much your particular mind can take. What is your capacity? When is there too much information to hold in one head? Why can't those of us filled to capacity hold up our hand and say, "I can take no more, please don't tell me anything else?" I can only retain my Visa number. I cannot also remember my password for PayPal and Twitter; my brain floweth over. I had my brain tested a few months ago by a psychologist and he said that I had very little RAM space so I can hold only about three numbers at once and I can't build an argument because I forget where I started. I have other problems with numbers. I once called my husband from South Africa and told him I'd gotten a house for a steal, for 10,000 rand ($1,000). I was three decimals off: it was 10 million rand ($1,000,000).

How much information are we supposed to be able to take in? I'm sure we're equipped to know only what's happening on our street and maybe the local deli—are we really supposed to know if there's been an infestation of cats in Malawi? If there's a flood in Poughkeepsie, what am I supposed to do? Fly over there, get in a canoe with a hand pump and start draining? OK, if you show me a photo of a maimed person, I will write you a check immediately, but most of the time, what are we supposed to feel about these global disasters? I would probably like to know if my next-door neighbor gets shot but maybe I'm not so upset if it's someone three blocks away. How close am I to the bullets? That's what I want to know. I feel terrible saying this but it's what I'm thinking.

I'm skeptical as to why people are so intrigued by worldwide atrocities. I know people who watch CNN all day, particularly when working out on the StairMaster, buffing their buttocks while those headlines of disaster slap them in the face with an up-to-the-minute report on another maniac with a gun gone crazy. You can see a lip-lubed anchorwoman running over to an injured bus driver shoving the microphone in his face demanding, "How do you feel about the incident?" giving him a little kick to keep him conscious. "How do you feel?" She has the look of a cat before it kills a mouse as she turns to the camera and says, "Well, Jerry, that's all on the up-to-the-minute report on the tragedy happening down here, back to you."

In some deep, dark way we all become salacious around a disaster; our mouths water slightly when there's a real emergency. Hurricanes, typhoons, wars, shootings, epidemics; we're a little aroused because now we really have something to think about rather than our monotonous lives; something to take the focus away from our to-do list. We have a little break to think, "Well thank God it's not me." Then we forget again after a few days and get on with worrying about the pickup at the dry cleaner and buying another light bulb. You can see the look of disappointment on people's faces when the report comes that the hurricane has dipped from three thousand knots to a light breeze. We all love a disaster; nothing tastes as good. The savage still lurks underneath no matter what we're wearing.

WE THE EMOTIONALLY INEPT

We have created rockets to the moon, computers that can . . . well, you name it, they can do it. And Starbucks on every corner of the world, but the other part of us, the emotional bit is still in the primordial swamp. Emotionally we are still on all fours, grazing our knuckles on the ground, looking out naively from under our one big eyebrow. Many of us don't even like to say the E word (emotion) because some of us think it is a glitch in this otherwise perfect human machine. Emotions are to be eradicated as quickly as possible like a blemish or a laugh line.

But it is these lurking emotions that cause us the most trouble, and we haven't risen above them. We're still slaves to them when they rear their ugly heads.

We used to hold in high esteem those who got the highest grades at school, and they went on to be hugely successful. (Times have changed. There's not some little guy at the top selling soap powder anymore, now most people need an MBA from Harvard just to put on their pants.) We've learned that the brightest might be the very ones who screw us the hardest. They know the math; they feel they can rob the bank. We used to trust these guys; we thought they were like Superman. To relax on weekends they go helicopter skiing in Alaska—no long run for them, they have to leap from a plane. To unwind, I chew a chicken bone in front of the television, they jump off a cliff.

Want my advice? If you're checking out whom you want to

do business with, ask what they do to relax on the weekends. If they say helicopter skiing, walk away; they are mentally not right. The most cognitively brilliant people usually have had to sacrifice their emotional selves. They live in a fog of facts, rarely creating a new one, just regurgitating everything they've ever learned and we're supposed to think that's smart. That's a walking Wikipedia, not a human being. This also might mean they're not top of the class on the morals front. They feel nothing so they can squeeze you dry without a wisp of remorse.

Envy

This is my weak area. Even if in terms of success, I'm cooking with gas, if I suddenly see someone with more, I get that kick in the stomach, that stab in my heart that means I want him dead. I am the first to step forward and admit, I want what the next guy has. No matter what it is, I want it. Sometimes I get the lust for things I don't even want. I'm so ashamed of this but in the throes of envy, if I accidentally pick up a gossip rag and see Lord and Lady Pomkelson Pompel Pomp sipping champers, with their smiling teeth yapping at some opening of something (I would shoot myself if I were actually there), I can't help feeling that old gutter-rat sense of envy bubbling below the surface. If you ever hear me say, "I'm so happy you got that job I always wanted," believe me, I not only want you dead but your whole family wiped out. I used to tear out pages of *Hello!* magazine going, "Die, die, die."

I'm always checking how many tweets other people have

compared to me, to make myself crazy. I look at Stephen Fry's Twitter when I'm feeling particularly suicidal. He always inspires me when I need my envy stoking up. It's like that spot on your gums that hurts when you stick a pin in it but you can't stop doing it.

If only humans had a cookbook to see what our ingredients are. We could look up "envy" and see that we all have it; it comes with the human package. It's just one of those things that kept us alive when we roamed the ancient savanna. It's part of the survival-of-the-fittest kit, so that if one *Homo erectus* had an attractive pointed stone, we all wanted it and so we made our own pointed stone or, even better, smashed in his skull with a stick and stole his. It is in our biology, this reptilian feeling of wanting what the next guy has. We can see it in the hubris of Greek drama. In every one of those plots, if someone got too big for their boots, divine justice would drop by and make them poke out their own eyes and then accidentally screw their own mother.

Rage

Your emotionally underdeveloped area may be anger, a very common ailment in the human psyche. It's left over from when we were basic grunt, kill, and mate apes. This is how it manifests itself now; you see yourself as a perfectly civilized person, law-abiding, popular with friends, and a respected citizen. Then something in you flips and triggers some alien rage that turns you from Jekyll to Hyde in a second: could be a traffic warden, could be your secretary who forgot to give you a message, could be your husband/wife who got lost again because he/she can't read a roadmap. Suddenly you're unrecognizable: lips back, teeth bared, a terrifying bark emitting from your throat as you verbally bully your victim to dust. You want to hammer them but the fear of prison holds you back by a thread. Usually after the incident you get the backwash: the poison you shot out comes right back at you and you suffer the hangover of shame and guilt until they drain from your system or you ask God to forgive you.

Deception

Don't be too hard on yourself; we are born with deception too. If we want something, we have the innate skill to manipulate the situation in our favor. We can hijack someone's shot at getting the job, partner, money, you name it. We have the ability to outfox. We know how to smile but underneath we are plotting to overthrow them; talking behind their back, pretending to be happy for them, and then hacking their phones. We are still animals under the skin; shifty and devious for survival's sake. Evolution has even provided facial expressions to throw people off the trail so that we can succeed with our deception.

Facial Expressions

Before we had words, we spread the news using our facial expressions, and to this day no matter where you are on the planet, even if you're born blind, by ten months you'll know how to pull up both sides of your mouth and smile; a real one, not that thing airline stewardesses do when they give everyone "bye bye bye bye" like they have a bad stutter. Nature in its brilliance made sure the first expression a baby learns is a smile because if it didn't smile we would have ditched that screaming glob of fat (who can't even go to the loo by itself). To this day people will tolerate and even love you if you smile. People in showbiz have this pummeled into them, singing to themselves, "Smile though your heart is breaking, smile even though you're faking . . . smile and the world smiles with you."

Whether you live in Bora Bora or Duluth, the facial expression for anger remains the same. It can be recognized by a drawing back of the lips and showing teeth, which demonstrates to others that you could eat them if pushed. The exposed teeth were to show how sharp they were. How white they were was irrelevant. The growling was dropped once we learned to swear. We show disgust by flaring our nostrils and putting our mouths in an "ick" shape to show others around us that, let's say, the fish is off. Fear is easy to spot: the openmouthed screaming and bulging eyes gives a big clue for those nearby to run. Surprise is an intake of breath with an open mouth, warning others that something is not as it should be. It could be something bad or good; it's sort of the human version of a warning light.

Laughter begins as a half scream from the shocked response of seeing something unexpected—a man slipping on a banana. You're about to express alarm but when you realize the danger has passed, that he's still alive, your lips draw up and your eyes crinkle to show others that there is no emergency. Humor comes from shock followed by relief, expressed by a barking noise. It indicates that this is a joke, not an actual catastrophe and the bark is so ludicrous, so infectious, that others around you also bark and clap their hands, all joining in the celebration that the pie in the face was not serious. Everyone is so relieved they bark some more.

We're born with the forty-seven facial muscles that create our expressions. All of our emotional states are viscerally connected to our facial muscles so that we can read each other loud and clear, underneath language. Watch a silent movie and get back to me.

We developed facial expressions not just to read each other but also to deceive each other. For example, if you found food and you didn't want anyone to get it, you could fake a look of disgust then everyone leaves and you get the meat. Those who were best at deception survived, and the suckers fell by the wayside. This remains the same today. The schadenfreude face is one of the ugliest of all expressions. It means, I'm-so-happy-sorry-but-mostly-I'm-happy-you've-been-demoted-or-even-better-fired. If you watch a face it will tell you everything. For instance, you cannot fake a smile. There is a muscle under the eye called the periocular that will not become active if you aren't genuinely smiling. The mouth is easy to upturn but if you don't find something funny, that periocular muscle just doesn't move; your eyes are dead as a trout's.

Learning to read faces should be compulsory in school so you'll be able to decipher what people are really thinking.

Imagine if we all could spot right off the bat when politicians are lying, they'd all be out of work in a week. Someone should have walked out of Bernie Madoff's office and screamed, warning others (with his mouth wide open and fear in the eyes and then flared his nostrils to show disgust). Then all those people wouldn't have lost $50 billion. If we were taught how to read faces, we could have spotted those sociopathic mortgage lenders and noticed they had the eyes of lizards.

Jealousy

I wish we could express jealousy like kids do. If someone gets something you want, you just hit them over the head and snatch it back. That's why children are so un-neurotic. They are doing what we only dream of.

THE ROAD TO WISDOM

First step on the road to wisdom is to face ourselves honestly. People used to call it baring your soul; I call it looking in the mirror and cutting the bullshit. Here's how I read the situation. You may see it a totally different way but I'm the one writing this book so it's pretty much going to be my opinion.

Because of this faulty plumbing, we're anxious, angry, fearful, stressed, and depressed, and we try to put the blame on what's going on in the world. We blame it on climate change, the Muslims, the Jews, the banks, whoever the enemy is at the time. They change every half an hour. Sometimes they have a beard, then they're wearing a dishtowel on their head, then in a bedsheet, I can't keep up. We blame whoever happens to be president or prime minister. The names change, they come and go; we hate them all. We love them in the beginning, then turn on them and say, "It's all their fault we're in a mess." But I say to you, we put them in there, we voted for them. The problem lies in us. We are always in conflict, and so that is how we see the world. The bully isn't out there. It's in here, in our minds. Inside ourselves there is always war and problems that will never go away until we declare a truce in our own heads. That's my speech on world peace. Over and out. Bob Geldof says, "We are the world." We are. He didn't mean it in a nasty way, but I do. It's all our fault; no one else is in the driver's seat, just us. Many people want to change

> **The bully isn't out there. It's in here, in our minds.**

the world; they don't want to change themselves. Wisdom isn't something they ever write about in *Vogue* or can sell at Saks Fifth Avenue. I wish it were; it would be so convenient while shopping for shoes. We used to have people we could ask these more existential questions. Where are they now? Out of work, like everyone else.

"Life is meaningless, God is dead." Oh please, I'm depressed enough. Imagine if Sartre did stand-up, the whole room would slash their wrists. Most of us don't have old Shaman grandmothers sitting on their haunches, breasts pointing to the floor, handing down their knowledge. My grandmother couldn't even tell me where she left her teeth, let alone the meaning of life.

We spend a whole lifetime hunting for some wisdom. In childhood, it's "happy days"—our biggest challenge is hitting the potty; after that, the shit hits the fan. By the time you reach your twenties you're fueled with the stress that you have to end up as someone special. Clearly some give up and just take root on their sofas but most young folks feel they have to turn on the turbo and go for the gold. In your thirties you're fighting to keep what you've got and by your fifties you know it's going to get taken away. And this is where the road divides and you turn into either wine or vinegar.

If you live long enough, a miracle might happen. If you make it to eighty-three and a half, just when you look like a walking Lucian Freud painting, you might become wise. But it has to be that late in the day: You cannot be a babe and wise, it's against the laws of nature. But if you make it to eighty-three and a half and you don't get overwhelmed by fear that makes you withdraw into your past, boring everyone senseless, and if your mind stays flexible and curious and you ask people questions and truly listen to their answers, and if you let all your narcissism, resentment, regret, and envy drain out of you, and you finally realize that the world will be fine without you, then you're wise.

My Search for Normality

Perhaps I've come across as too negative in the book so far. I assume that what I'm writing about is our general malaise; what all people feel deep inside. I might be wrong, I've gotten things wrong before and I'll admit I'm not an expert on what normal people feel if they indeed exist. So I apologize if you're sitting there going, "What the hell is she on about? We don't think about any of these things. We live a happy and healthy life. Let's give this book to Uncle Psycho."

I didn't mean to insult any of you. On the contrary, I am a great admirer of people who believe they are normal; I am fascinated by them. I've always thought, Is it possible to feel the way Tony Robbins looks? Confident, positive, flowing with love for himself with his big wall-to-wall teeth and large genitalia. (I am guessing about this but he has a very large nose and I connect the two.) What makes him so sure he's right? Does he really believe the script that is pouring out of his mouth? Is that normal?

I obsessively eavesdrop in public places (bars, trains, buses, restaurants) with my ear almost in the fruit salad in my search for who might be normal. I listen in to a conversation in a bar where a seemingly normal group of good old boys, teammates who work together, making valves for garbage disposals, are all out to celebrate the up-and-coming plumbing awards for which they have gathered. They seem so content with their lot; a happy pack at the watering hole, clinking glasses, toasting one another for the fact that they're up to win "Plumbing Team of the Year," fantasizing their names are being called out, hitting the air with their fists as they hear in their heads the music playing "You're the Best," then each one of them makes a little slurry speech about how they couldn't have done it without their team, posing for an imaginary photo, giving each other slaps on the back. Is that normal?

I've listened in on a girl at the next table in a restaurant, panting with excitement as she asks her friend to be her maid of honor at her wedding and the friend bursting into tears and rhapsodizing on about how she'll be the best maid of honor that ever lived and can't wait to help choose the napkin color. . . . Is that normal?

I sit in a hotel lobby and listen in to two cigars with fat men on the ends yabbing about the price of housing, throwing out percentages of the increase or decrease of the market with complete confidence about how right they are. How does anyone accurately know how much a house price is going to rise or fall, and who cares? Is that normal?

EVERYONE'S AN EXPERT EXCEPT ME

At dinner parties, I hear people locked in debate about how to resolve the crisis in the Middle East like they're experts. "Here's what I would tell the Taliban." The president couldn't figure it out with his advisers but these "if you ask me" people presume to know. They base their extensive knowledge on the same newspaper everyone else reads; yet they have the answer. Where does that confidence come from? Around the world everyone is an expert. There must be at this very second sixty-four billion experts having coffee and giving their opinions on climate change, nuclear disarmament, obesity, and the war on drugs.

I sat next to a man telling me what the Flemish were thinking during World War II. I was dripping in sweat thinking, "Should I know that information? Will he think I'm an idiot when he finds out I know nothing about the topic and is there going to be a quiz?" I don't even know where Flemmark is. I have to sit there, dying inside with self-loathing, while the Flem expert whips out more information I didn't ask for.

This exhibiting of memorized fact is how we unconsciously determine who the alpha is at the dinner table. Lecturing on Flemland to people who have no idea is the same as the chief gorilla beating his chest to show who's boss. This Flem guy somehow senses that I know nothing, and I'm sinking in a mound of self-hatred, so he feels triumphant—he's won that round until he meets a bigger expert on Flem matters, at which point he will immediately attempt to change the subject.

People find their scrap of knowledge and unquestioningly live their lives gathering their little pile of research then boring people senseless with the details.

To be honest, the main reason I listen in is to find someone, someday who might come out with an Earth-shattering revelation and I will scream, "Aha! Bingo! That is the answer to why we exist." It hasn't happened yet but I'm always on the lookout. My suspicion is that we're all wondering what normal feels like;

all believing the next guy knows but not us. This may just be the way I think so forgive me if you don't agree. I do know that we all want to be happy and we spend a great deal of our lives hunting for the key. No matter how powerful or successful we get, we still can't figure out how to deal with a mind that keeps us up at night, driving us to exhaustion. This isn't just for those who are considered mad, it's for all of us. I wish we could just come out and say how we really feel; I know I'd be so relieved.

PART TWO

WHAT'S WRONG WITH US? FOR THE MAD-MAD

DEPRESSION—BROKEN BRAINS

'm going to start with my own story as throughout my life I have had ever-increasing episodes of depression. I hope others can identify even if they don't have the full-blown illness. We are all, at times, at the mercy of our more compulsive and fearful emotions and have no means to find a way out.

MY STORY

It was World Mental Health Day and I was asked to go on the BBC World Service to talk about depression. I happened to be suffering very badly but didn't want to say so, even though I was talking about the need to end the stigma. I was wearing sunglasses during the interview and should have taken them off and said, "Do you want to see what depression looks like? Here it is." I was too ill to think that far out of the box;

my only concern was getting through it without breaking down on air.

As soon as I finished the show, I asked the driver to take me to my doctor, at a rehab facility called the Priory, to up the dosage of my medication. This had already happened a few years earlier when I had depression while filming a TV show and insisted on hiding it. The show was about various mental illnesses and each week we would film at my house. My doorbell would ring and there would be someone with ADHD, schizophrenia, OCD, bipolar disorder, bulimia, physical dysmorphia—you name it, I had them over for tea. The problem was, during the first few shows I happened to be in the Priory, and I didn't want anyone to know for fear of losing my job. My husband would pick me up; all the other patients looked at me like I was crazy (high praise from the experts) as I was driven home to interview someone with a mental illness without saying a word about how sick I was. When it was over, my husband would drive me back, and I'd get back into my pajamas and go to bed.

I'm wary about harping on about depression. People glaze over; you can see them thinking, "Oh here she goes again, jawing on about 'the darkness.'" Once you couldn't say *gay* and before that it was the C word and further back you couldn't even mention you were a witch—depression is the latest taboo.

And this isn't something that happens to a small minority; it's up to one in four of us, so where is everyone? If it's not you it's probably a relative or a friend—everyone knows someone. When Hamlet says, "O, that this too too solid flesh would melt thaw and resolve itself into a dew!" That's got to be one of the most accurate descriptions of depression. (If a shrink heard you say that he'd have you on meds in seconds.) Part of the stigma lies in the fact that the word *depressed* depicts a kind of

> *Depression doesn't care if you're famous, if you live in a mud hut, or what culture you come from, it just loves everyone.*

"down in the dumps" sentiment. Sadness or unhappiness is perfectly normal if something has not turned out the way you wanted it to or someone has died.

Depression is a whole other beast; it is not situation appropriate. Here's something you get absolutely free with this illness: a real sense of shame; it comes with the package. And you feel such extreme shame because you think, "I'm not being carpet-bombed, I don't have anything to complain about." Your thoughts become so punishing for your selfishness—like bombs, incoming over Dresden—so loud, so relentless you get not one voice but about a hundred thousand abusive voices; like if the devil had Tourette's. Depression doesn't care if you're famous, if you live in a mud hut, or what culture you come from, it just loves everyone.

Those of you who do suffer know that we just need to look in each other's eyes, and we recognize that we have the illness. It's like a secret handshake. You can read depression loud and clear if you look into the eyes of a sufferer; there's no mistaking it—it's the look of a dead shark. Most people don't really look closely so they'd miss this detail. Teachers should be trained to notice that look in their students to get them help before the cutting starts or worse, a suicide.

MY STORY

Here's a coincidence. I'm having a bout of depression right now as I'm writing this book. So I'm going to just write down my experience as it happens. If it were an acute episode I wouldn't be able to type these words; I wouldn't be able to connect one thought with the next or even comprehend the meaning of words; I would bury this computer in a closet, sit on a chair, and wait to be institutionalized.

Luckily, due to practicing mindfulness, I have an early warning system. It can't eliminate depression, but I can hear the alarms before it eats me alive. This is why I can continue to write. I'm aware I'm just in the foothills of depression, but I can hear the far-off footsteps of the negative, derogatory thoughts creeping up on me.

There are clues that something is wrong because I can sleep only two hours at a time and when I wake there is dread; heavy like a weight on my chest. My movement is limited and trips to the shower are like getting ready for a decathlon. I have to pep talk myself up with, "Come on, Ruby, you can do it, one step at a time. It's just your illness, it's not you. You will come back, it's just an illness." And then of course I'm aware of the infamous to-do list, which starts like that giant round boulder chasing Harrison Ford in Raiders of the Lost Ark. I try to figure out why I feel the cannonball compulsion to go out and purchase things on the list. I try to question the thinking that tells me, "If I could only get through that list, I'd be fine."

Another mental torture arises from the fact that I'm being haunted continuously by the thought of how old I am and how many years I have left. I have been doing this periodically since I was forty; now I do it all the time. Each day I look for signs of my decay and, in finding them, feel my own imminent death.

I'm also becoming obsessed that I need to buy blue-and-white-striped cushion covers. (The shame, the shame.) I have spent six hours on my computer scanning for nautical covers, and I hunted some down in Canada and some in Mexico; it took me four more hours to figure out how to use the credit card, I was shaking so much. Some have actually been sent to me and they are too tiny, much tinier than in the photo on the website, and cost £93. I want to send them back but am paralyzed by the certainty that I don't know how to do that. Now I am consumed with self-loathing; I spent all that time choosing them and now they look like bits of tissue paper with stripes; cheap, awful. I am left with a picture in my head of my ideal striped cushions, fixating about where I can locate them.

I already had this obsession recently about lamps. I had arrived in London, and I actually made my taxi driver stop on the way back from the airport as I leaped across busy traffic, nearly being hit by a truck on my way to a lamp shop. It didn't have exactly what I was picturing so I leaped out another six times. I told the driver it was an emergency (what emergency could be happening in Habitat?). I finally bought a round plastic garden lamp, which is all wrong. It changes color and looks hideous. So I'm still on the lookout for a lamp but now I also need those cushion covers. I had been in Ireland for work, which was why I was coming home from the airport, and I hadn't seen my children for a long time. What am I doing? I'm jumping from shop to shop to find lamps. Wouldn't you hate yourself if this were you?

The feeling is that of being a corpse, no sense of skin or other extremities, like fingers or legs. I'm this empty thing now and honestly have no recollection of the chutzpah I had only last week. Now nothing is anything, and everything is nothingness, just the cannons of pressure going off in my head. It's as if your old personality had been sucked out so slowly that you didn't notice its departure. Very slowly it's been stolen away, and each day you remember less and less of who you are and what you feel.

I want to try to go to another store but I know I will get there and wander like a nomad, lost and unable to remember why I went. This is why people think depression is something you make up; how could I convince someone that my thoughts are bombarding me with household goods? This could be why there's a stigma—anyone in his right mind would say, "What the hell is wrong with you? Why would we give money for researching a cure when the problem is getting a cushion? Am I supposed to take that seriously?" They'd say, "Come on, people are dying of cancer. They wouldn't know a cushion if it came up and spoke to them." I want to tell them that the voice telling me to get the cushion is the illness. People don't commit suicide because they can't find a cushion but the feeling of helplessness, the sense that your brain does not belong to you anymore, with its insane commands, could drive you over a cliff just to get some quiet.

As I say, I am only in the foothills and simply noticing what my thoughts are gives me whole seconds when I know that those thoughts are the illness; they are not me. So I am in the depression, knee-deep, not over my head yet. I'll keep you posted, though you might know anyway because this book may never get written.

Next Day Still Depressed

I'm writing again the next day, and yesterday after the unsuccessful hunt for the lamp and cushions, my girlfriend Kathy asked me to come over for dinner along with (I kid you not) the former prime minister and a handful of other luminaries. While Kathy's asking me over, I am on the Internet looking at a cushion.

In the old days, at this point in my depression, I would have run upstairs to get dressed, thinking I needed to meet these people for some reason. I would have brushed aside the fact I was ill, jumped in my car, and driven, wild at the wheel, sweat-

ing, probably getting seriously lost and almost crashing several times before finally arriving and trying to look nonchalant. Then I'd drink too much to overcome my fear that they'd see I'm an idiot and suss that I know nothing. They would be talking about the Labour Party while I would be internally vomiting trying to add something enlightening. The evening would end with me drunk, nearly in passing-out state, trying to be funny, taking over the room and slurring about how much I loved my dead dog. Somehow I would find myself at home without knowing how I got there and think about suicide.

Next Day

So another day passes and I get up exhausted remembering that my TED talk goes live on air today, and I'm at level ten of anxious; assuming that no one will watch it and those who do will think TED is now getting idiots on. I'm feeling like I'm walking toward the lions in the Colosseum because I know that however great I should feel about being on TED there will inevitably be that wrenching agony just around the corner that they will pull it off the air because I get a unanimous thumbs-down from the viewers. I know that whenever something good happens or I've actually accomplished something and feel a glimmer of pride I am pretty much immediately kicked in the ass by karma. Also, today, most important, I decide I have to have a white carpet to match the cushions. I had one, which is now missing and I am screaming at every-

one *in the house because I am convinced someone stole it. "Where is it? Who took it?"*

I am now Googling carpets, ignoring my children who want to tell me something, but I have to find the perfect one, and when I see one I like, I use that tiny magnifying glass on the photo that lets you see the pile up-close with a hand stroking it (just a hand, no body) up and down, as if you could feel it yourself. I'm judging how it feels and then move on to another site to imagine feeling other rugs.

At this moment my only relief is the image of the blue-and-white-striped cushions; when I think of the blue I feel calmer, otherwise I cannot see colors, the world inside is black and white. I wish it were an image of something inspired or sacred rather than a cushion, but I'm telling you this only to you give an idea of the obsessive, mind-numbing weight of this disease.

Fingers crossed I will find the cushion, the lamp, and the carpet.

Facts About Depression

- The current annual economic cost of mental illness in the UK is £70 billion, which is equal to the entire national health budget.
- By 2030, the World Health Organization predicts more people will be affected by depression than any other health problem.

- It already affects more people than all physical illnesses put together.
- The World Economic Forum estimates that the global cost of mental illness will be about $16 trillion by 2030. Unipolar depressive disorders are the third biggest global burden in the world.
- Mental illness affects people early (50 percent of cases occur by age fourteen).
- Mental health problems also increase the risk of physical illness. People with schizophrenia and bipolar disorder die on average sixteen to twenty-five years sooner than the general population.
- At any one time, 10 percent of the U.S. population has experienced clinical depression in the past year, and between 20 and 25 percent of women and 7 and 12 percent of men will suffer a clinical depression during their lifetimes.

WHAT DO WE DO ABOUT DEPRESSION?

So here's the million-dollar question: What do we do about mental illness? If therapy and drugs are working why is it on the increase? And how does a GP know how to make a correct diagnosis in ten minutes? Each one of us is different. And we are so complicated, how would they find the right cocktail for you? It's a zillion-to-one crap shoot, especially as the drugs themselves are archaic (taking an antidepressant is like burning down the whole forest because one tree is diseased), but at the moment they are all we have.

Fellow sufferers have asked me how to deal with their illness. Here it is. This is what I would say to anyone who has a mental illness themselves or has a family member, friend or co-worker who is suffering: Tell them to find someone else who has what they have, whatever the illness. They are not hard to locate: They are one in four of the population, remember? You don't need to be Sherlock Holmes.

Half of the cure is realizing that you are not alone, that this illness actually exists like any other physical illness; you are not making it up and you are not a self-indulgent, self-obsessed narcissist who's looking for pity or an excuse not to show up at work or school.

> *Half of the cure is realizing that you are not alone.*

Find someone who shares your pain. Go and locate what I call a "fucked buddy"—someone you can always call, day or night, when you can't take it anymore.

If you talk to people who don't understand they will nod and say how sorry they are and tell you to try to get better but they cannot feel it and will eventually get bored or, in extreme cases, leave you. (So many people have told me that they've been abandoned when they were in the depths of depression.) If you find someone who has what you have, they will never get bored; they will talk drugs, voices, and heartache with you till the cows come home. They will relate and resonate with you, holding your hand through the agony.

MY SUGGESTIONS (A DIATRIBE)

Alcoholics Anonymous has a system where you call your buddy when you feel you want a drink and they will talk you down. Why can't we have meeting places like in AA, where they all get together for their twelve-step thing and have cigarettes and cookies? How did they organize these get-togethers so well? They have meeting places on every corner of every block; more places than there are Starbucks. How did they figure all this out? Why can't we do that? We're similarly discriminated against; if you ever write that you suffer from a mental disorder on your CV, good luck landing a job. It should be against the law, just as it is with someone physically disabled.

The gay community turned it around in my lifetime; now they're everywhere: politicians, CEOs, generals, movie stars, hairdressers. . . . Let's go find where they keep their old rainbow banners, high-heels, and tutus that they wore during gay rights parades, put them on and march to the White House with pitchforks screaming, "WE ARE MENTALLY ILL. WE ARE THE ONE IN FOUR AND PROUD. CHANGE THE LAWS. WE ARE LIKE EVERYONE ELSE." Maybe if we do this we won't have to hunker down in isolation anymore, quivering in case someone we know finds out, or, worse, someone at work finds out, and we're either dismissed (the company probably will say for other reasons) or treated like a person with the black plague. OK, that's my suggestion. Take it or leave it. My political rant is over.

REALITY OF MENTAL ILLNESS: IN THE BRAIN

Depression is the result of something going wrong in the brain. We perceive the world outside only because of our brain: everything you dream or create, what you laugh or cry about, hope for or imagine, who you worship or love, whenever you dance Zumba, pole vault, make pumpkin pie, hold up a bank, it is all because of some activity in the brain.

I'll give you a few examples of some of the physical ramifications that affect your behavior if you get whacked in any specific region of the brain or you suffer from a tumor.

If, for example, you damage an area in the temporal lobe it may result in a syndrome known as prosopagnosia, or face blindness. This means you will no longer be able to recognize people's faces. So your mother may be standing in front of you and you will have no clue who this woman is, even though you can see her clearly. (Some days I wish I had that problem.)

Capgras's syndrome is also caused by damage in the fusiform gyrus but in this case you are under the illusion that your mother is an imposter. You would say this person looks like your mother but it is not her, it is someone identical. This is thought to happen if brain pathways that connect the face-processing areas to the limbic system (amygdala) have been severed or damaged. If your mother called you on the phone you would recognize her voice but if she were standing in front of you, you would not believe it was her.

Another example of cross-wiring in the brain producing abnormal behavior is known as synesthesia. This can be genetically transmitted with the result that your senses are tangled. If, for example, someone plays a D note on a piano, it might be perceived as yellow, or E is experienced as maroon. Others can see numbers as colors. They say Einstein had this; it must have been a psychedelic light-show in his brain. Again this is not a result of imagination but because of damage or genetic factors.

Another syndrome known as pain asymbolia, also due to miswiring, has the result that a person responds to pain with uncontrollable laughter. Another person with pica disorder will eat things that are not edible—rocks, buttons, toys, doors, watches, blue-and-white-striped cushions (God forbid).

Damage to the right hemisphere of the brain may affect the left side of the body (the right brain controls the left side of the body and vice versa). If you have brain damage on the right side, you will not attend to what is being held up in front of you on your left side. Both eyes would be fine—it's just that your brain would not process any information in the left visual field. In really bad cases you'll ignore the left side of the world. You will only eat food off your plate on the right-hand side and leave the food on the left. If you are a woman you will put lipstick only on the right side of your mouth. (This can be incredibly funny but it's best not to laugh at people with this syndrome. If you must, do it on the left side because you won't be seen.)

Then we have the very bizarre somatoparaphrenia. This is when you're unhappy with a certain part of your body so you ask to have it removed, such as an arm or leg, usually not your head. You have the delusion that this limb or side of your body does not belong to you. You are aware of it—it just doesn't seem to be part of you. This one requires a real hard bump on the head, stroke, or epilepsy in the right hemisphere, especially the right temporoparietal junction, which is also the region responsible for so-called out-of-body experiences. So the experience that you are floating above your body, watching it from the outside can be repeatedly evoked by stimulating this part of the brain in a laboratory. How many tickets to India could have been thrown out the window if people knew they could get this buzz in a lab?

Here's my personal favorite disorder: Cotard's syndrome. The sufferer claims he or she is dead. If you look at his brain in a scanner, you can see where the damage is that causes these thoughts. All senses become disconnected from the emotional centers in the brain; nothing has any emotional resonance so there is a complete cutoff from any reality. And so the person will assume they are dead. If you prick them with a pin and they bleed they will be surprised and conclude that the dead also bleed. A hundred years ago, the sufferer would have been called crazy or, before that, burned at the stake.

Here's my point: If Cotard's syndrome is considered a neurological malfunction that causes the sufferer to feel dead, why is depression, which shares the same circuitry and symptoms, not taken seriously. It's a no-brainer.

Vilayanur Ramachandran (to me, one of the most impressive of contemporary brain scientists) has done extensive research on these disorders and found that schizophrenia could also be described physiologically. Based on work he's done on anosognosia, caused by right-hemisphere lesions or damage, he has discovered that the sufferer becomes unaware that they are ill or impaired. They may be blind or paralyzed and believe that they are perfectly fine as they walk into walls. What's interesting is that anosognosics share the same symptoms with schizophrenics who cannot distinguish between what they think or imagine and what is really happening in the outside world, so that if they were imagining they were Marie Antoinette and were unaware of external reality, they might actually believe they were her. When schizophrenics move their bodies, they often can't tell if they are moving it themselves or it is being moved by someone outside themselves; which means they might come to the conclusion that perhaps aliens or Jennifer Aniston were in charge.

Brain-imaging research, using PET scans, EEGs, and fMRI (functional magnetic resonance imaging), can explain why one guy is normal in every other way except that when he sees his uncle he sees a giraffe. Now you can just scan him and have a look. There it is, the reason for the odd behavior or hallucination, clear as the nose on your face.

The brain (the actual organ) and the mind (moods, emotions, thoughts, memories, personality traits, and all the information carried by your neurons) are intrinsically intertwined; they are codependent. If the brain is damaged so is the mind, and alterations in brain chemistry cause changes in moods, memory, and attention. So why is there such a stigma when it comes to mental illness when we know it is caused by genetics, disease, trauma, or physical accidents?

MY STORY

About five years ago, I wrote a comedy/tragedy called Losing It *with my friend Judith Owen (she wrote the music, I wrote the script). I had recently become the poster girl for mental illness, though in the past I wouldn't have mentioned I had depression, let alone written a show about it. The reason I was able to be open about my illness was because I was unintentionally "outed" when Comic Relief asked me to pose for a photo to raise money for the mental health arm of their charity. I assumed it was going to be a discreet small stamp-size photo in the back of some magazine.*

Imagine my horror when I walked into a tube station and saw a gigantic poster of me with "This woman has mental illness—can you help her?" written underneath. I was mortified and hurled myself onto the poster to hide it but there were too many so I kept hurling to no avail. I suddenly had a flash-bulb moment: I decided to write a show and pretend the poster was for my publicity. I thought, "Ruby, if you've got a disability, use it." I wrote the show and toured mental insti-

tutions for two years; if you can make a schizophrenic laugh, believe me, you're halfway to Broadway.

The show was performed at more than fifty mental institutions around the UK; the Duchess Theatre, London; the Menier Chocolate Factory, London; and the Purple Cow at the Edinburgh Festival. At this point it evolved into my one-woman show, Out of Her Mind, and played at the Broad Stage, Los Angeles; the Theatre on the Bay, Cape Town, South Africa; and the Forum Theatre, Melbourne, Australia.

I still perform the show but my interest has dramatically shifted. I decided I would look into the actual brains, which make us how we are because it really is the most interesting thing in the universe. Much more than the stars up there—they can look after themselves or Brian Cox can take care of them. Who is "us?" That is the mystery. As I had just mentally imploded, this was probably the perfect time to address it.

Back to School

So I thought, I'm eighty-seven (not really), why not go back to school but this time listen and not get expelled for putting sardines under the lighting fixtures? OK, I'll start over again. So I enrolled at Regent's College of Psychotherapy. On day one, I loved my new friends. I'd carry books like I used to in high school, piled high in my arms, and we'd all go to the cafeteria and get in a queue for awful and hard lasagna and neon-pink dessert on a tray. I loved that. And no one treated me like I was even interesting. If you don't think of yourself as special, no one else does either. People notice you only when you want to be noticed. Watch a famous person: They almost shine a spotlight in their own faces even though they pretend to want to be ignored. At the end of the day, we'd do group therapy, and some of the more dominant girls and I formed a clique and we'd gang up on the weaker men. We'd roll our eyes and grunt whenever they spoke. Our circle got tighter as we defended each other saying we were strong not aggressive, working as a unit of bulldozers.

Weird things still happened as they did in my past. There were about sixteen people in my course and they were a diverse bunch. One of my classmates had been a hooker in the past (I loved her). Now she wanted to help people rather than screw them. What a gal. It turns out she recognized one of our fellow students (a guy we hated because he was smug and sanctimonious) as being one of her ex-clients. Of all the people in the world he had to walk into that place and then into this class. The ex-hooker told me this in confidence; I guess she felt she could trust me to keep quiet. I kept my mouth shut for three years and, my God, was that hard when he belittled women. I never said a word and I still haven't: I'm writing it down.

But I loved my course. Each week we studied another great therapist, and I believed each one, and then the next week disbelieved him and went on to my next shrink crush.

Freud: Brilliant with the unconscious and what a concept that underneath your lid is the id, the furnace of hell *that lies beneath all our frilly fronts. It is the ego that keeps up appearances, it's sort of our psychic underwear so we don't have to face the world exposed as the pathetic mess we really are. (I once had a Freudian analyst with whom I argued about a cigar being just a cigar. He wouldn't have it and told me I only said that because my father made sausage casings and that was why I was so screwed up. He kept trying to make me delve into the fact I have a recurring dream that I'm sitting in a box in the desert, covered in blood and feces. "It's no big deal, everyone has that dream," I told him. Also I told him about the dream I have where I am on a plane and the tail breaks off and we have to land in a narrow alley with the wing tips making sparks on the brick walls, ending up in a quaint ski resort in Switzerland. What's to figure out? I settled my bill of £5,000 an hour and walked out showing him who was boss.)*

Melanie Klein: *She believed that Mommy had a good and a bad breast and that could influence the mental condition of an individual. I obviously got the wrong breast, the evil one. (I forget if it's the right or left one.)*

Carl Jung: *I loved him and the idea we have a shadow, a dark side, and was so happy to find out it was a real address.*

Carl Rogers: *I also loved person-centered therapy. Rogers just reflected whatever you said back to you like a parrot but with love. You would say something and then* he'd say, "Do you mean . . . ?" followed by exactly what you had just said. Simple.

Gestalt: The acid trip of therapy. You get screamed at about what a fake and loser you are and somehow this helps you find the apple core of you, if you haven't had a nervous breakdown in the process. Not dissimilar to primal scream therapy where you relive your birth again but this time you're tough enough to take on your mother even if it's only the womb.

Then came the existentialists, each more upsetting than the last:

Heidegger: What a guy. He wrote total gibberish putting dashes between-every-word-you-read, seeing-thou-as-a-being-in-the-world-not-an-it. If you address someone as "thou" it means you really like him and acknowledge him as a fellow human. If you think of another person as an "it" it means you are just using him to get what you want; he is a means to an end. This cleared up so much for me as far as sorting out the "thous" from the "its."

Nietzsche: Impossible to spell; another colorful guy who said, "God is dead" and we shouldn't raise our hopes.

Winnicott: I also loved him. He talked about the "good enough" mother so I felt that he excused me for almost killing my children when I accidentally fed them rat pellets. He said that as long as the mother meant well, the *kid wouldn't turn out to be screwed up. Thank you, Winnicott.*

Bowlby: *Gave me all I needed to know as to why I was and am mentally ill. He divided caregiver–baby relationships into three types of attachment categories that exemplified your relationship to the world and to yourself. There's secure attachment when Mommy and Baby are in tune, googling away at each other. When Mommy leaves the room, Baby cries and wants her back, and when she returns he goes to her for soothing. Ambivalent attachment is when Mommy leaves the room and Baby just sits there looking bored, and then when she comes in looks even more bored and plays with some blocks. And then there is disorganized attachment, when Mommy leaves the room, Baby looks relieved, and when she comes back, he screams. Guess which one I was?*

To attain full qualification as a therapist, you have to work for four hundred hours as an intern. I got to two hundred and people were still asking me if my clients laughed when I came in the room to be their therapist. Actually, when I got my first client I was more nervous than I've ever been; I thought, what if they scream, "You're a phony. I don't like you, get me someone else." My concern wasn't that they would recognize me, it was the same fear that anyone new to the job would have: "What the hell do I say to this person?"

Actually they didn't recognize me or care who I was. They had bigger problems. A few of my clients were women who were held as slaves by their husbands' families and threatened with death if they told anyone. I sat there and thought what an up-my-own-ass spoiled brat I was to have ever thought I had problems. These mothers-in-law who splashed boiling water on their daughters-in-law to show who was boss made my mother seem like Tinker Bell.

And the ones that were English, even if they recognized me, couldn't care less because they could feel that we had a lot in common. They'd talk about their loneliness and hopelessness, and I really listened with compassion, which is the main point of shrinkdom. I felt it was an honor that they let me into their lives, and I still wonder if I helped fix them, at least a little. I learned that we're all such delicate creatures and many of us are in pain and it takes such bravery just to go on living.

I realized after working two hundred hours that I was starting to lose compassion and I could never fake it. I think you either have to be insane or an angel to sit there and hold all that incoming pain. As it happened, perhaps just to test me, I was offered a bite at show business again while I was still working with abused women. What did I do? I grabbed at it like an addict finding a fix. I still shudder at the memory and shame of what I did. You would have thought I had learned my lesson from the Shark Attack incident, but no. I was asked to do a big prime-time game show, where I would be the master of ceremonies in a circus tent while F-list celebrities performed trapeze work with no net. A panel with some screaming queens would judge who was the bravest in this gladiatorial bloodbath.

I thought everyone concerned would know how grotesque this all was, and I could poke fun at the desperate celebrities hanging by their toes to make a comeback or, in some cases, risking their lives to emerge from the cocoon of mediocrity as fully winged TV personalities. Sadly this was not to be. They dressed me in a corset, gave me a whip, and sent me into the ring. I was told to take it seriously and not to make fun of anyone, to keep my irony to myself. I was left without a comedy life raft as I had to say how magical the starlet was while she was hanging above me by her cervix, wearing a feather. I wanted to say how amazing it was that she had just come out of rehab but they made me shut up and say, "Let's hear it for her, ladies and gentlemen. Give a round of applause to this remarkable woman."

I read the teleprompter with tears pouring down my face while cranked in a hideous smile, eyes dead. Well they fired me, which was a lucky thing because I was still working as a therapist. At supervision sessions, where we went each week to get feedback on our work, the supervisor said maybe it wasn't a good idea for me to be a therapist at this time. I asked why.

She pointed out that I was on billboards throughout London half the size of a football field wearing a corset with my breasts in 3-D hanging out of the picture and holding my whip; that perhaps some of my clients might think it strange. Perhaps she had a point.

So I thought, let's leave psychotherapy to the psychos and get into the meat; I'll learn how the brain works. I crashed a neuroscience course at a big deal University in London filled with twenty-one-year-olds. I felt like a freak, so I told them I had a skin disease; that one where you age really fast? Then they let me go out with them until they realized I really was old. Eventually the fetuslike students included me at lunchtime, mostly because I was the only one who drove and I could take them to the park.

The only science I had done was at high school when I once dissected a frog and put it in my friend's handbag, so I didn't come with a lot of credentials. There I was every week with my notebook, scribbling down how some sodium molecules pass through the synaptic wall by an electrical current, thereby transporting neurotransmitters to the next neuron, which happens more than a trillion times in less than one-thousandth of a second. I didn't know what they were talking about but I took hundreds of pages of notes, all incomprehensible scribbles now. I could publish the notebooks and call it The Art of a Madman. In the end, the rest of the class went on to Yale University to complete their master's. I remember them all waving me farewell because (a) I was only crashing the course and (b) I knew very little.

I thought, I've got to trump them going to Yale, so I did the only thing I could think of, I got into Oxford.

In years to come, anyone consulting the class of 2012 photograph from Oxford University's Kellogg College will see among the dignified students looking earnestly into the camera, a very immature (in attitude, not years) student look-ing demented with happiness—that would be me.

My children are furious because I left and went to univer-sity before they did—let them find out what the empty nest feels like. I heard one say, "Our mother's left home. She's at freshers' week and we can't find her." Before even the first class began, I had to do something called matriculation. I had no idea what that word meant—it sounded like an infection—but the next thing I knew, I was in full bat cape and square hat walking with hundreds of other students down Oxford High Street with locals cheering. I waved like the queen. As a student who never got the hang of spelling, you can imagine how startling the experience was.

You file into some ancient building and then the dean of deans, dressed like a grand magician, welcomes you by say-ing, in Latin, "Welcome! Now you are in the most holy of holy institutions." At that point, I could think only that if I could dig up my parents and they could see this, they would never be-lieve what was going on. Their heads wouldn't just spin, as the saying goes, they would fall off.

It was very strange to me that I suddenly started reading science books so voraciously at this time in my life. It was as if my old self had died and been taken over by a nerd. When did I turn into this? It seems I had reinvented my new self into a groupie for neuroscience; a fanatic follower. So after two years at Oxford University, here is my spin on neuroscience.

PART THREE

WHAT'S IN YOUR BRAIN/ WHAT'S ON YOUR MIND?

WHY NEUROSCIENCE?

In order to get to know who you are and how you work, you need to metaphorically open the hood and look in at the engine. Freud, who originally wanted to be a neurologist, had to guess what was going on inside because in those days the only way you could study the brain was by hanging around a corpse. A dead brain is not ticking so it doesn't help. Now we can look in and see how neurons connect to different areas of the brain and watch the electrical and chemical power working throughout to create our thoughts, dreams, hopes, memories, emotions—everything.

We are the result of those connections, those chemical exchanges and of regions communicating with other regions. Some people believe this thinking is too reductionist and say disapprovingly, "Is that all we are?" I feel we should be saying, "Oh my God, I am all this?" Because what we are is so complex and extraordinary; how our brains work makes every other invention and accomplishment look like learning to fold a napkin.

For me, this has been the greatest aha! moment to end all ahas in my life so far. When you begin to grasp how every part of your brain has a function (valuing, thinking, moving, feeling), when you realize it's the subtle (and not so subtle) differences in our brain biology that make you you and me me, you'll go aha! too. Then you'll think, "We absolutely must have the instruction manual for this thing," and you might even start stalking neuroscientists like I did.

As far as reality checks go, it can't get better than having a look at the real thing. Each one of our brains looks fairly similar when you crack us open, which to me is so comforting; to know I'm not alone and that we are all brothers under the skin. No light versus dark souls; just a dull pink. The best news of all is that we have reached a point in our development as a species where we can choose how our brains will react to events so that we're not held entirely captive by our old habits and biases, programming, and mental blind spots. Most people don't know that this self-regulatory part comes with the package. We're born with this ability but sadly this information isn't imparted to the public (perhaps it wouldn't sell as many books as *Seventy-Five Shades of Grey*).

When you learn how to use your mind as it can be used, you might even feel that elusive thing called happiness or peace. Yet what is known so far in terms of brain science doesn't seem to trickle down to the masses, nor does the public seem to want it to trickle. Scientific information about the brain is based on hard evidence from a number of sources, including, most recently, advances in neuroimaging. These provide vivid pictures of the brain's components and associated functions. Neuroscience as a subject is still on the nursery slopes for the most part, as it is extremely complicated, but scientists have already learned a huge amount about the functions of our brains and the different areas involved when we add numbers, speak, make decisions, remember, hear, see, and stay busy. If you doubt the empirical evidence but you do believe you've seen a UFO, please put this book down. It is not for you.

By watching how our thoughts affect the structure of the brain, we're learning new ways we can consciously reshape our own brains. Self-regulation means we can actually rewire our own brains by moving activity from one region to another, switching on diverse hormones that can stimulate us or calm us down.

In my opinion, learning this ability to self-regulate is the posttherapy zeitgeist. It has become the new holy grail of our time. Evidence of how the brain changes can be seen in brain-imaging scanners, and the results are published in scientific journals. Why isn't this the hottest news in town? You meet people who insist they know how the world works and themselves by how they feel. It's like insisting that the world is flat because they feel it is. I know change is painful to us all; old ways are always being replaced by the new. Soothsayers suddenly found themselves out of a job and alchemists were made redundant because people stopped needing their pigs turned into gold, or whatever it was they did. Someday we will laugh our heads off when we remember that a doctor didn't look inside your brain before he wrote you a prescription. I'm not saying that by simply looking at an image in a scanner we'll know everything there is to know, because it is true that who we are is also the result of our interactions with our parents, our environment, our learning, and our culture. So to get to the bottom of the twenty-first-century problems we find ourselves facing, we'll need not only to learn about the basic functional architecture of the human brain but also our personal story and our evolutionary story.

Here, based on scientific evidence, neuroscience, and evolution, are some answers to the questions raised in Part 1. Enjoy.

WHY THE CRITICAL VOICES?

We have this proclivity for negative, nagging voices in our head because of that old fly in the works, survival. Every cell in us wants us to last long enough to pass our genes to the next generation, then we can go to hell as far as they're concerned. Part of our brain still thinks it's four hundred million years ago so that we're on the constant lookout for predators who once killed us. Even in a resting state your brain is still tracking the horizon because back then there was so much lurking and we could do something about it, like run. Now, it's not enough to just run from what we perceive as threatening; we're helpless in the face of twenty-first-century danger: economic bedlam, out-of-control climate, and far-away countries that might be hiding bombs. No wonder we're stressed.

This is why we're overvigilant with paranoid feedback: "Look out for that . . . Don't screw up . . . Those people hate you." You're reacting just like your cat that hunches his back and hisses, but you're hunching with words. It's the anxiety that keeps you on your toes. Close your eyes for a second, take your eye off the button, and you're lunch. You can see why a glass half empty is our natural state.

The brain detects negative information faster than it does positive. We are drawn to bad news. When something is flagged as a negative experience, the hippocampus (responsible for consolidating memory) makes sure it's stored in an easy-to-reach place for future reference. If you whistled a happy tune and just thought lovely thoughts, you'd probably be hit by a truck pretty quickly and find yourself as road kill. This negative bias primes you for avoidance and fear, but when you direct it at yourself, it can bring you to your knees with depression.

WHY DO WE NEVER HAVE ENOUGH?

Science tells us that the reason we "want" is that we are driven by a chemical in our brains called dopamine, and when we get something we want, we reward ourselves with a hit of it, which creates a buzz, a kick, a thrill. It's like cocaine (which I never tried but heard about from other people, I won't name names, but I was told it is the same high). If you lust after something very badly (say a pair of shoes) and then manage to buy them, you get a dollop of dopamine, which motivates you to immediately start planning how to get the next pair. (This insane version of forward-planning was handed down from when we foraged for nuts or whatever we foraged for hundreds of millions of years ago. We'd find nuts, eat them, and then immediately start making mental roadmaps of where to find other nuts in a similar terrain to the one we just scored. We probably didn't even notice we were eating the nuts because we were so busy thinking about our next forage.)

But back to shoes. These days with the ants in your pants from the dopamine, you'll need to find out how and where to get more shoes so you'll begin to close in on shoe-rich environments—that is, malls. You'll start sniffing around Jimmy Choo shops and might even empty your bank account to buy some, and the more you make that connection between malls and buying Jimmy Choos, the more entrenched and deeper that habit gets. After a while even if you just smell a Jimmy Choo shoe, your dopamine will run riot. If you go to a fancy dinner party and someone is wearing a Jimmy Choo shoe, you're now so primed to "get shoe" that you might gnaw her foot off to get that buzz of excitement back again. With dopamine it's the craving; that's what drives you, not the actual shoe. It's the chase—the thrill of the hunt driven on by cues in the environment that predict the next shoe around the corner. Dopamine does not always generate pleasure but impels you to seek rewards. You can be a very unhappy addict.

If, on the other hand, you don't get the shoes, the dopamine decreases in your system so you start to get feelings of withdrawal similar to going cold turkey from a drug; you get all itchy and scratchy like everyone does in *Breaking Bad*. It's like we have a meth lab in our basement. You're informed about this by a part of your brain called the basal ganglia, which acts as a thermostat, registering stimulation coming in from the senses. Once the hunt becomes less novel you lose that motivational "oomph."

At first, the basal ganglia is your best friend; it gets you high, you're cooking with gas, you want to party but when you can't get enough, *boom*, you're a junkie on skid row. We are our own walking pharmacies shooting ourselves up with homemade chemicals. This constant need for a fix to make you feel good prompts you to pursue rewards over and over again and strengthens the behavior that made you want to get them in the first place. It's a vicious circle.

So the reward system is necessary for your survival; you can use it for positive effect in order to increase your motivation for the healthy feeling of satisfaction for a job well done. But it can also push you so much into overdrive that it will run you ragged in your desire to achieve the unachievable. We need to be aware of each of our individual tipping points to differentiate between when we are on a high of creativity and production and when we are burning the engine. Our culture promotes an endless need for fulfillment to always want what the next guy has, even though the effort might kill us.

A LITTLE HISTORY OF
HOW THEY FOUND OUT
WHAT'S WHERE IN THE BRAIN

Having answered some of the questions raised in Part 1, I am going to name names as far as the mechanisms of the brain go, so that when I discuss mindfulness in Part 4 you'll see how you can intentionally change the physiology of your brain (neuroplasticity) and thereby regulate your thoughts and feelings.

In 1861, the French anatomist Pierre Paul Broca opened the brain of a patient (after he was dead) who could speak only the single syllable *tan*. That's all. Imagine going on a date with this guy—repetitive or what? Anyway, Broca noticed a lesion growing toward the back of the frontal lobes and suspected this damage might be the cause of the speech problem. Broca decided that this must be the area responsible for speech and called it Broca's area. Tan couldn't argue. All he could say was, "Tan tan tan." A tragedy.

After that it was like a gold rush. Everyone started to open everyone's head to find out what part was responsible for what. They all wanted to get a piece of the action and name some real estate in the brain after themselves. It has never been a dream of mine to have a tumor named after me, but the next guy to get famous on discovering a lesion was Wernicke who, in 1876, found an area below Broca's area and he claimed that damage to this area was why one of his patients (another dead fellow) couldn't string words together. He knew the words but could not create a sentence that made sense. So his patient would say "catfoodgaloshesheadmakecakeonmyhands." Obviously, he couldn't argue with Wernicke, so this area became known as Wernicke's area. To recap, Broca was the discoverer of the "no speech" area and Wernicke was in charge of the "not being able to string a sentence together" zone. It's a good thing the two patients never met. It would have been a dull party.

From this, neuroanatomists went into a frenzy and found that right across the top of our brain, from ear to ear, all humans have a somatosensory cortex where the brain receives signals from points on the surface of the body and registers them as touch. God knows how they found this out. I don't even want to know, but this is where the brain registers the sensation from every part of the body. So if you stuck a pin in the area in your brain that represents your third toe you would feel pain in your third toe. In this somatosensory cortex there is a whole map of every region of your body not in the order of your parts from your head to your toes, but rather in order of what areas are the most sensitive.

This goes for every single area on your skin: an elbow area, thumb area, and genital area all have plots of real estate up in this somatosensory cortex where they can be felt. The size of the area relates to how many nerves you have in the specific

A REPRESENTATION OF THE
HUMAN BODY PROPORTIONATE
TO EACH REGION'S SENSITIVITY

region; the genital area and land of tongue are huge, because they are highly sensitized, while elbowville is not so huge. The county of shoulder—teeny. It's as if your body parts are getting bigger plots if they're used; genitals and tongue the size of Texas, armpit is Chattanooga.

If you had your foot amputated, you would still feel it in the foot neighborhood of your brain, thanks to a syndrome known as "phantom limb." And if certain parts of your body become injured or diseased, neurons will grow to compensate for the missing part. What I love most is the fact that because the areas for the genitals are near the area for the feet in the somatosensory cortex, some people have reported that they feel they're having an orgasm in the area of a missing foot. Once these discoveries about the brain's wiring were made, all such bizarre syndromes started to make sense.

After this, neuroanatomists found and investigated movement maps of the brain. One such map was the motor cortex, which runs from one ear over the top of your brain, like headphones, and each point controls a different part of the body. So rather than receiving incoming sensations like in the somatosensory cortex, the motor cortex sends signals out, telling certain areas to move. If you stick a pin in the motor cortex area for your knee, your knee will twitch. If you stick the pin in the hip zone, the hip twitches; it may be possible to stick pins in certain parts of someone's head and make them walk like a chicken.

But back to science. It was also discovered that if you stuck a pin in one area of a person's cortex and his finger twitched, that if you then stuck a pin in the exact area of another person's motor cortex, his finger might not twitch but his lip would. This is proof that each person is not created equally. Your cortical maps are all different sizes, depending on which part of your body you use the most and the least; the more developed parts have larger corresponding brain regions.

The man who discovered this was a real hero of neuroplasticity: Michael Merzenich, a postdoctorate fellow at the University of Wisconsin-Madison.

He found that if you're a pianist and you practice moving

your fingers up and down scales, hour after hour, day and night, more neurons would grow in the motor cortex of the finger area of the brain and expand its topography. I used to have a piano teacher who slammed the lid down while I was playing if I made a mistake, which is probably why I confess to war crimes whenever I see a piano. If you were a flamenco dancer you'd have more real estate in the toe area of your brain. Someone who licked stamps for a living would obviously have a larger tongue terrain. Do you see where I'm going with this?

When you're building up clusters of neurons by habitually moving certain parts of your body, it's like building muscles when you pump iron. In both cases the movement gets easier and more automatic because that area gets stronger. Of course, neural exercise doesn't give you bigger pecs or a six-pack, so you have to choose brain or brawn. It's very rare to have both. (See Arnold Schwarzenegger.) But there's more than one way to be attractive and looks aren't everything, or so I tell myself.

WHAT'S GOING ON IN YOUR MIND?

First let me say we've come such a long way from where we started. From a one-celled amoeba, a tiny pinheaded thing clinging onto a rock, to an evolutionary orchestrated master-piece; our brain, which looks like a three-pound piece of tofu. This jellylike substance has more horsepower than every super-computer that ever was, squared. It has two hemispheres and

various lobes, each of which plays a crucial role. Zapping
throughout our inner landscape are approximately a hundred
billion neurons, electrically transmitting information, sending
it at the speed of light throughout our whole nervous system.
These hundred billion neurons can have anything from ten
thousand to a hundred thousand branches or dendrites or connections (for the less bright), and every time you learn and experience something, they get better at firing, and the wiring
gets denser, creating a serious forest of brainpower. I have heard
it said that the brain is capable of more connections than there
are stars in the universe (how they counted this I have no idea
and maybe they're making it up). It's hard to believe that each
and every one of us carries this equipment, even reality TV
stars. What a waste.

And yet we still have many glitches; we are not *Homo perfec-*

tus yet, far from it. We all basically have similar problems since we share the same plumbing. We all have cracks. We just hide them from each other.

Our brain has been shaped by evolutionary pressure over time to provide our bodies with ever more efficient ways of surviving and reproducing. It is designed to process all information for the purpose of living on, it doesn't care about happiness—it has things to do, places to go. So you may want to just swim with dolphins for the rest of your life (and some do) but most of us are primed to be busy: to go get, to provide food on tap and a roof over our heads in order to be able to get the best mate possible for gene purposes. (Google "trophy wives and sugar daddies.")

THE TRIPLE-DECKER BRAIN

The cause of much of our confusion is that we actually have too many brains in our heads. Three to be precise. Starting with the oldest brain, the other two newer ones are outside it like Russian nesting dolls; a brain within a brain within a brain. Unfortunately our old reptilian brain didn't get absorbed; it's still in there squashed with the newer models, like a relative you can't get rid of.

This ancient brain, developed about four hundred million years ago, is called the brainstem; it is the "duh" part of the brain. It prompts us to mate, kill, and eat, which is perfect if you're living in a field or working at Goldman Sachs.

Then around 250 million years ago, the paleomammalian brain (but that's way too long a word), or limbic system, came online; that's where we, unlike reptiles, were motivated to bond with and nurture our offspring, rather than eat them. (Not such a bad idea when you think about school fees.)

During our neomammalian phase, about five hundred thousand years ago, we grew a superior brain, the prefrontal cortex; the executive brain, El Capitano. This provided us with the tools for self-control, consciousness, awareness, language, and self-regulation. Also for rational, strategic and logical thought; math; and morality. It is the gatekeeper to the primitive brain, so if you suddenly want to eat without a fork, it will inform you that it isn't such a good idea. Same with peeing in public. The brain tripled in size in the last three million years (which of course is a blink in the history of us), and we suddenly got the ability to feel sorry for each other and acquired cooperation skills like group hugging. (See New Age.)

This mishmash of three brains, called the lizard-squirrel-monkey brain, all trying to function at once is one reason why we're nuts. This is why there are women who read Heidegger but who also want to screw the plumber.

I will explain where things may have started to go wrong for us: errors thanks to evolution. Millions of years ago, when we were ancient man, as I have said, we were perfectly fine and at one with our environment (no one had panic attacks or OCD). When we met a predator and felt danger or a threat, we'd fill up with our own adrenaline and cortisol to take on our foe. Kill or be killed. Have lunch or be lunch. After the ordeal was over, we'd defuel and the chemicals would go back to normal.

The problem these days as modern man is that when we perceive danger, adrenaline shoots into us but because we can't kill a traffic warden or eat a real estate agent, the juice never comes back down. We're in a constant state of red light alert, like a car siren that drives you nuts.

Because we can't kill people who anger us, we have all this pent-up rage. To make things worse, when language came on-line, about seventy thousand years ago, we started to use words to describe those constant feelings of alarm, so everything was perceived as an emergency. Now, it wasn't just, "Oh, there's a sabre tooth tiger," it was, "Oh, I forgot to send that email," "Everyone hates me," "My thighs are too fat," "I didn't get invited to the Christmas party." This is what drives us mad: the never-ending voices.

The thing that helped us survive in the past (our alarm system) now gives us nervous breakdowns. Someone said, "Man was built for survival, not for happiness." Sorry to be the bearer of bad news but our pets are happier than we are. Cats, happy happy. Dogs, happy happy. Human beings, screwed. Completely screwed.

A LITTLE ABOUT STRESS

These days we are more likely to die in different ways from our ancestors. We (in the West) no longer have to worry about scar-

THE STRESSED BRAIN

let fever, bubonic plague, or cholera. In the 1900s, the big diseases were tuberculosis, pneumonia, and influenza. A person living through World War I was more likely to die of flu than in battle. Now because we're living longer and better than ever before, we slowly fall apart.

Out on the savanna, our physiological responses were perfectly suited to deal with stressors (run from the big animals with big teeth). These days we can't just run from what drives up our anxiety and stress: mortgages, money problems, looking hot, relationships, and deadlines. Evolution did not set us up to suffer *Jurassic Park* levels of stress, day in and day out; that's the bitch of living at today's pace.

You say, "Oh, come on, you lightweight, we can deal with stress, bring it on." It isn't the stress that makes you sick or even your risk of being sick. Stress increases your risk of getting diseases that make you sick, or if you're already sick and you add stress, you can kiss farewell to your natural defenses. The fact we can't switch off our alarm is what makes us vulnerable. So here's my point: stress-related diseases are disorders of excessive stress responses. (Take it or leave it.)

As I said before, you can be the creator of your own stress without any outside influence. As soon as you even think about stress, a whole cascade of reactions happen: Your thalamus (the relay station of your brain) sends out a wake-up call to your brainstem; signals are sent to all your major organs and muscle groups, getting them ready for fight or flight; and your adrenal glands release the stress hormones. Cortisol suppresses the immune system to reduce inflammation from any injuries and stimulates the amygdala to keep you vigilant, which produces even more cortisol. It also suppresses activity in the hippocampus, reducing your memory so that you think about only what you did last time you had a similar emergency. Eventually, the actual neurons in the hippocampus (where some of your memory is stored) will burn out; the more you stress the blanker you'll get. Ever study insanely for an exam and the next day go blank? You've burned out your memory for the sake of a test.

With mindfulness, you learn to regulate these chemicals, intentionally increasing the ones that promote health and happiness and decreasing the ones that don't.

This chemical also stops your digestion and the urge to have sex. (Although there are some people who like to have sex during a hurricane.) Thinking about sex or eating during a disaster would only make things worse. Another chemical, epinephrine, increases your heartbeat so it can move more blood and dilate your pupils (to help you find your foe in the dark). All this is useful if you're actually in danger. If you're not actually in a life-or-death situation and those chemicals can't stop pumping through you, they will wreak havoc on your body and brain. Excessive chemicals eventually inhibit your immune system (the defense against infections and illnesses), making you vulnerable to viruses of every shape and size. They will lower the production of serotonin (making you feel listless and joyless as in depression) and can eventually, if they remain virulent, contribute to heart disease, hardening of the arteries, type 2 diabetes, obesity, infertility, premature aging, and certain cancers. Inadvertently stress will destroy you both mentally and physically unless you change the way you think about it and relate to it.

With mindfulness, you learn to regulate these chemicals, intentionally increasing the ones that promote health and happiness and decreasing the ones that don't.

MY STORY

As someone who suffers from depression, I decided to take up mindfulness as an antidote to this very harmful buildup of cortisol. We can't get rid of stress entirely, so this practice is a way I learned to deal with it. When my emotions get too high, whether it's elation or distress, I have to come back to a baseline or I'll literally be flooded by my own cortisol, and swept away by depression. Because I've had so many episodes, I need only a few drops of this toxic chemical and I'm vulnerable to its effects. Before doing a show, I use mindfulness practices (see later in Part 4) to cool my engine so that I can take the hit of adrenaline that comes with the job and use it to my advantage. If I'm too up on stage, I'm anything but funny. I become a desperate woman with those pleading, fear-filled eyes. I know myself better these days and can succeed only if I work from a level of calm to make creative thinking possible, otherwise my head fills with the "everyone hates me" school of thought. If I'm calm, I can think on my feet, my eyes lose their desperation, and creativity flows. This

*doesn't mean I'm in a blah state, it just means I'm keeping my
eye on my speedometer so I can step on the brake or acceler-
ate when I need to. For me this is done with mindfulness, not
wishful thinking.*

PARTS OF THE BRAINS: THE EASY-TO-UNDERSTAND VERSION

"Let's start at the very beginning, a very good place to start." I
like to quote Julie Andrews when discussing neuroscience. The
pattern of how neurons or cells are wired together determines
the way we think. Whatever we experience mentally is a result
of the different combinations of neurons. As I said earlier, each

neuron can link up with ten thousand to a hundred thousand neighbors and make connections. The parts that join up are branches or dendrites (which receive incoming information) and axons (which send signals).

The inside of your head could be compared to Las Vegas, where every experience, sensation, thought, and feeling corresponds with billions of electrical lights zapping on and off like a stadium wave on a gigantic electric grid. Your ability to do everything—including your dreams, hopes, fantasies, fears, and most of all your ability to read this book—is created by neuronal connections, chemicals, and specialized regions in your brain calibrated by your genetic history, your development, the society you're born into, and of course, Mommy and Daddy.

Neurons transmit information to each other via electrical impulses not dissimilar to those used to jolt Frankenstein's monster up from the gurney and make him kill people. When a neuron fires, an electrochemical wave ripples through it, on its way to signaling the next neuron.

You may have learned this at school, but I will remind you that the neurons don't actually touch each other; between each of them is a tiny gap, called a synapse, across which chemicals are passed (called neurotransmitters). When neurons become excited through enough stimulation (because of a thought or experience), an electrical wavelet fires down the length of the cell to activate or inhibit the neurotransmitters. At the other side of each gap are little receptors, like flowers opening to pass the chemicals across the synaptic cleft and lodge in the next neuron. Once they cross over they create an electrical zap that sends an electrical message to the next neuron. This is how neurons communicate with each other through electrical and chemical impulses—and those babies can go from speeds of two to twenty miles per hour. The whole process is not dissimilar to a game of hot potato but electric. Just think, all this is going on inside your brain, right now and you're just lying there without knowing it. You should get on your knees and thank evolution.

Learning is about new neurons connecting together; memory is made possible by those changes happening over and over again to embed the new pattern. When neurons fire many times because you're memorizing a new fact and you study it again and again, your synapses are actually changing their shape to speed up receptiveness and increase the firing, making them more efficient at passing information in the future. Learning has happened because of the synapse changing shape, and the longer the shape is retained, the longer you hold that information. Use

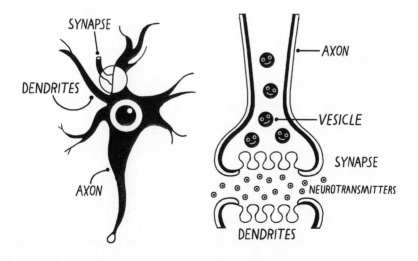

it or lose it. If you repeat a mode of thinking or behaving, the pattern of the neurons becomes strengthened. Neurons that fire together, wire together. When they don't fire, the connections eventually just shrivel and die like the Wicked Witch of the West melted when they threw water on her.

Your average neuron fires five to fifty times a second, meaning there are zillions and zillions of signals traveling inside your head right now carrying snippets of information. The nervous system moves information exactly like your heart moves blood. All those zillions of emails zapping around in your head are what define the mind, most of which you will never be aware of. The number of possible combinations of a hundred billion neurons firing or not firing is ten to the millionth power, or one followed by a million zeros. (I'm just trying to show you there's a lot going on in your head.)

As more and more complex skills became part of your repertoire, from rubbing sticks to make fire to building a rocket, more and more neural cells connect and grow, and these dendrites or connections become stronger and stronger and more and more synchronized in their firing patterns. If you learned Mandarin, you'd get a whole set of synchronized neurons in the language department, or if you take up banjo, a whole bunch of neurons are lighting up in your brain in your finger area on the somatic map in your brain. Whatever you're doing or thinking about is reflected in areas lighting up in your brain, and you can watch this firework display during brain scanning.

Everything that happens, every thought, feeling and perception you have, changes your brain, and those changes are how you learn things, from bowling to dumping your boyfriend. However, the brain isn't just a mass of unspecialized information processors; it has distinct regions that do specific jobs.

Neurons (with their shooting neurotransmitters) form into pathways and multiple networks with specialized functions and via these pathways the regions are able to communicate with each other, the way a subway system works going from station to station. All information processed by the brain is nothing more than electricity passing through neuron after neuron with little squirts of juice across their gaps. (Not very glamorous sounding, I know.)

Genes

I can hear you ask, "What about genes? Don't they play a part in all this?" No one knows how much your genes contribute to make you who you are or how much your experience shapes you. Nature (referring to genes a person has inherited) or nurture (influenced by environmental factors)? It's a toss-up. Genes hand you a deck of cards; how you play them is up to you. A gene is a unit of hereditary information linked to one or more physical traits: leg length (I'm furious I will never go

> *Genes hand you a deck of cards; how you play them is up to you.*

down the catwalk with what I've got), blond hair (another thing I wished I had), and larger lips (a must for my modeling career). Your genetic code (the blueprint of you) is contained in your

DNA and informs each and every cell where to go (which is why your ear doesn't grow out of your foot), so your DNA is like a traffic cop, directing trillions of cells, determining what each cell actually becomes, and killing off those that make a wrong turn.

Genes create proteins, and they can turn that gene expression on and off, up and down. In the brain, gene expression influences levels of neurotransmitters, which influence functions like intelligence. This is why some people get A's without working for them (I hate them). Or they influence memory, for those who win quiz shows about general knowledge (I hate them too).

The environment also influences gene expression, so how your brain works and who you become depends on diet, education, and the color of your wallpaper.

We have around thirty-one thousand genes, and they don't all get switched on, no matter what Mommy and Daddy passed on to you. Good news for those of you with crazy parents. You might be just fine, depending on your experiences. Some behavior is more heritable than others; you might start off with some genes loaded for depression, but they don't just switch on without environmental input. No one knows if you become you because of nature or nurture; it's a combination of what you're born with and how you live your life.

In our early years we are vulnerable to bad environmental experiences, so Mommy and Daddy can seriously damage your gene expression. Each baby is, in the first five years of her life, at the mercy of her parents' download . . . and they got their downloads from their parents . . . and all the way back to the baboon and beyond. (It's a miracle we're not still swinging from trees. Next time you see royalty, just picture their forefathers squatting in the bush.)

The brain is divided into four lobes. Form has function and I'm going to tell you about it, at least all that I know.

Just a note, the brain is much, much more complicated than my humble descriptions; many regions overlap in their functions, and cognitive neuroscientists spend their days figuring out what each of the specific regions do. In a way, they're still in the dark and so am I. The following is just a broad sketch—so if you're a neuroscientist don't bite my head off or any one of my lobes.

FOUR LOBES: EACH LOBE HAS A RIGHT AND LEFT SIDE

Occipital Lobe

The occipital lobe is responsible for most of our visual processing. We don't actually see the world through our eyeballs; instead light shines through the retina and sends projections to different groups of neurons in the occipital lobe, each one specialized to interpret various components of visual information. For example:

Color

Orientation

Shape

Light and shade

Face recognition

This lobe works in conjunction with other regions (parietal and temporal lobes) that are organized into streams of visual information, such as the "what" pathway determining if it's a chair, cow, or your mother and a "where" pathway telling you, in your house, in the yard, on your face.

So, contrary to popular belief, it's not your actual eyeball that sees the world; you have a whole production company in the back of your head beavering away, producing a movie, creating the illusion that what you see is real. It's a film called *Reality* rather than actual reality. So many things are going on back there in the occipital lobe, and this is how you can remember a face or a scene and say, "Oh yes, I remember who you are, didn't I marry you ten years ago?"—something I've been known to say to my husband. Now I know why.

Temporal Lobe

The temporal lobes, located around the ears, gives you surround sound (auditory perception) and provides you with your ability to comprehend language and meaning (hello, existentialists), carries out emotional processing (in the amygdala), and is the home of specialized "explicit memory" centers such as the hippocampus. When there's a strong emotion during an experience, chances are you won't forget it thanks to structures in your temporal lobe. Say on your tenth birthday you saw a horse fall off a cliff and you became hysterical. That magic photo opportunity will be locked in your long-term memory thanks to the temporal lobe. Emotional memories stick the longest. That's why when you're memorizing history in school, you should picture yourself in the Battle of Hastings and pretend to lose your legs. You won't forget it then, I promise.

Parietal Lobe

The parietal lobe integrates sensory and visual information, so that you can navigate with a sort of internal compass to tell you where you are in space and give you a sense of being in your body. It then coordinates your movements in response to objects and tells you where and what they are, constantly updating the information as you move and interact with the world. This navigation system is a must to stop you from crashing into the furniture.

Frontal Lobe

The largest of the brain's structures is the frontal lobe. It is what makes (most of) us civilized and creates our personalities; it is the big boy of mental ability. This is the seat of our emotions and allows us to understand how someone else is thinking and feeling. It can plan a whole scenario so we can rehearse an outcome before we initiate it. Among its list of accolades are some of these babies:

Decision making
Problem solving
Judgment
And, best of all, emotional impulse control or self-regulation

RIGHT AND LEFT BRAIN

Corpus Callosum

The two hemispheres are connected by the corpus callosum, a bridge made of a densely packed band of nerve fibers shunting information back and forth and facilitating a continuous dialogue between the two halves; if this didn't exist, your left side wouldn't know what your right side was doing (and could play very cruel tricks on it). Luckily, it can seamlessly create the illusion that you are the result of one brain rather than two. Each hemisphere controls the movement in the opposite side of the body.

Contrary to popular myth, the right brain is not just the female feeling part of the brain and the left, the macho business side. It's more complicated than simple ladies' and men's signs on restroom doors: These two sides took hundreds of millions of years to develop, and evolution wouldn't come up with something that flimsy. The two sides share many features, and yet at the same time each side has specialized processing systems. Each side seems to compensate in strength for what the other lacks. The right isn't good at grammar so the left is spectacular at it.

The right is touchy-feely to get the big picture, while the left is better at reading, writing, and doing arithmetic and sweats about the details.

Perhaps from early in our evolution one side had to have narrow focus to find food (left) while the other side (right) had to be on the lookout, vigilant at watching out in case we were jumped.

Some Skills of the Right Side

Not great at grammar or vocabulary but fantastic at picking up intonation and accent

Creative

Intuitive

Skilled at putting pieces together (great at puzzles)

The home of autobiographical memory—the story of you

Picks up metaphors and jokes

All the information from the right is then sent to Lefty for interpretation.

Some Skills of the Left Side

Linear

Logical

Able to plan

Accurate and able to think literally and retrieve facts

In charge of vocabulary

The area responsible for those internal voices (boo hiss)

The narrator of your ongoing personal life story

The region where list-making lurks (boo hiss)

The left side is more densely woven with closely packed neurons, making this side better at doing intense, detailed work. These left-brainers are brilliant but can be very boring people. If there's too much left-brain, analytical, and logical thinking, you may not be a very warm and cozy individual. They make great businesspeople but are not always great fun. Asperger's-like symptoms (though less pronounced) are an advantage for these folks who need to focus on one particular thing and everything else can go to hell. Some people think this gift of pin-size focus is an asset in the information age. Left-brainers can sit for hours staring at a screen and nothing outside interferes.

Ideally the two hemispheres work together and make a perfect couple—that is, if the right gets a vibe that there is something dangerous outside then the left defines what it is. Creating a coherent narrative of your own life story involves the integration of the two hemispheres. Too much in the left you've got a boring accountant, too much in the right you get someone who talks to angels and probably can't pay the phone bill on time.

PARTS OF THE BRAIN: PART TWO

Right under the corpus callosum is the limbic system, the more ancient mammalian part of the brain. This part is good news for survival and motivation and bad news for civilization. Too much reaction from the limbic and not enough prefrontal cortex keeping you in check, and you might turn out to be a thug or similar.

A Few Parts of the Limbic System

Hypothalamus
The hypothalamus is involved with the translation of conscious experience into bodily processes; you think, then you move. It's also involved in hormone regulation. Here are a few of the processes controlled by the hypothalamus:

Hunger
Thirst
Body temperature

Sexuality

Blood pressure

Sleep

Thalamus

The thalamus makes a wake-up call to the brain stem (the duh part of the brain), sending signals to all major organs and muscle groups (like a call center that redirects incoming traffic to the appropriate area) and, if need be, gets you ready to rumble or run. All sensory information (except smell) is passed and processed through the thalamus. It's thought to be involved in consciousness because if you lose power there, you'll find yourself in a coma.

Hippocampus

Shaped like a seahorse, the hippocampus works like a search engine to locate and retrieve other memories quickly and smoothly, like a great secretary who knows where all your life is filed away.

Amygdala

The emergency alarm of the brain, the amygdala, sends responses to various parts of the body from emotionally relevant information. It coordinates physiological responses to get you ready to fight or run and makes sure you remember it for next time.

A Few Parts of the Frontal Lobe

Prefrontal Cortex

The "higher part" of the brain is the prefrontal cortex. It helps with assessing and choosing the correct social behavior (it's the "pinky up" part of the brain when you have tea at the Ritz) and has numerous other talents:

Higher thinking (planning, reasoning, judging)
Self-regulation
Impulse control

Anterior Cingulate Cortex

The anterior cingulate cortex (ACC) is the overseer of attention. It monitors predictive errors and conflicts, such as the distance you are from your goals. It is the basis of working memory; a workspace where you can gather information and solve problems and make decisions. It's also where actions are planned. The ACC comes into its own when you:

Gather information
Solve problems
Make decisions
Plan actions
Fulfill your intentions
Self-regulate

The ACC doesn't develop until you're between three and six years old; this is probably why kids have hissy fits.

Orbital Medial Prefrontal Cortex

The orbital medial prefrontal cortex regulates information from the external and internal worlds, especially in relation to reward. Its inhibition function can say, "Whoa boy," to the amygdala before it sends out the full alarm to "kill or run" or other embarrassingly primitive reactions, such as defecating on the carpet or having sex in an elevator. Using these reins makes you polite even when you want to chew someone's head off.

Somatosensory Cortex

As mentioned earlier, the somatosensory cortex is a region in the brain that has a map of all your body parts. The map isn't in order from your toes, knees, and thighs up to your head. It's in the order of which parts are the most sensitive, so the lips are right next to the genitals (an R-rated anatomical joke).

Insula

All those internal "vibes"—the feeling of butterflies flapping their wings in your stomach or knives in your heart—come from the insula. This area gives you a visceral weather report from inside. If you sense these feelings and link them with the ACC, you can then reflect on them and consciously make a decision if you want to pull the reins or not. (I'll be discussing this later because the ACC is responsible for self-awareness and regulation, which are strengthened by the practice of mindfulness.)

Cerebellum

The "small brain" at the tail end of the big brain leading to the spine is the cerebellum, which is in charge of balance, posture, and coordination.

Basal Ganglia

The basal ganglia is an area involved in motivation, motor selection, and action. It controls everything from big muscle movements to the flicker of the eyes caused by surprise, novelty, cravings, or drive. It uses our memories and translates them into motivation and then action. If it were to be removed, you'd be more like a doormat. (*Don't try that at home!*)

The Chemicals That Make You Who You Are

You know the expression "It's just the hormones talking?" This is usually said in a derogatory way to women who are having their period. Just because I have threatened people with a buzz saw through their car at this time of the month, I am categorized as hormonal. But ha-ha, it's not just us. Men, children, even pets are at the mercy of the hormones that dictate their moods. When you fall in love, it's not because someone sprayed fairy dust on you, it's just a hormone within that has been switched on. Think about sex. That's OK I'll give you a few minutes. It gets complicated, but to give you an idea, when a thought occurs it sends a message to your thalamus, which emails the pituitary gland, which in turn phones the adrenal, which sends hormones responding to the original thought. Maybe we're all just different recipes; recipes with legs. When someone asks how you are, you should just hand him or her a list of your ingredients. This is far more accurate than a star sign if you ask me.

Here are some of those ingredients and their main functions. There are more than one hundred different agents known to serve as neurotransmitters and many of these have different functions in different regions of the brain.

Serotonin

Serotonin is the feel-good chemical. People who have a lot of this in their systems aren't people pleasers. They feel good just being themselves. I have very little of this; I have to buy it over a counter. Your doctor can prescribe an antidepressant, so you don't have to suck it out of a friend's neck if you're low on it. It can turn anxiety into serenity and optimism, but it also affects other areas: appetite, blood pressure, and pain levels.

Dopamine

As I've said, dopamine motivates you to seek rewards. Cocaine does the same thing, but it's more expensive. Dopamine switches on (the basal ganglia lets you know you're running low) when you anticipate getting what you want, which is why the chase tastes better than the kill; it lights up under the scanner when we know we're just about to get our object of desire. Experiments on rats have shown that they'll give up food, sex, and rock and roll just to get a hit of dopamine. That's how good it feels, and rats are no fools.

Those driven, ambitious, A-type personalities are high on (perhaps among other things) their own dopamine, so they keep it on a constant drip, always seeking situations that jack it up a notch.

Noradrenaline

Noradrenaline is also called norepinephrine. It influences sleep and attention; it excites, alerts, and arouses. This is your "get up and go" hit. It starts your heart racing and blood rushing, but too much noradrenaline, and you find yourself in fight-or-flight mode. When a squirrel lifts its little head and jerks it around to look for trouble, he's on norepinephrine.

Acetylcholine

A shot of acetylcholine would make you whizz through university exams; it promotes attention, learning, memory, and neuroplasticity and is critical for control of muscles by motor neurons (it also keeps your heart pumping, so you don't want to go to empty on this chemical). When acetylcholine is released, near the brain stem, it enables neurons that are activated to strengthen their connections to one another.

Endorphin

Endorphins reduce pain and stress and create a sense of whoopee! by suppressing shame, vigilance, and self-criticism so now you can dance on tabletops in your underwear with a flower in your nose.

Oxytocin

When oxytocin switches on, you'll feel all cozy and milky like the perfect mommy. Very important to have while raising children; without it you'll want to run in the other direction when they make noise. When you reach out and touch someone, your oxytocin is lactating. Those with a lot of oxytocin could be described as cuddly, wanting to take care and metaphorically breastfeed everyone. In the queue of life they're always at the back taking care of others. (I have very little of this drug.)

Glutamate

Glutamate is the brain's CEO as far as exciting the neurotransmitters and forging links between neurons via the synapses. It's the most stimulating neurotransmitter for learning because it changes the way synapses work, thereby making it easier and more likely for them to fire. The more they fire the more engrained new knowledge becomes. The parts of the brain that use glutamate to communicate the most are the cortex and the hippocampus. Take out the hippocampus (a scientist did this by accident to one unfortunate guy) and you have around a thirty-second memory. (See Goldfish.) No glutamate and you can't lay down any new memories at all. Knock out the genes for glutamate receptors in mice and you get mice who will never find the cheese again. (I'm not suggesting you really do that.) If you give mice more glutamate receptors you get supermice that are going for their second PhD.

Vasopressin

Vasopressin supports pair bonding, attachment, and monogamy. It decreases aggressiveness in males and turns them into caretaking and intimacy-seeking creatures who write Valentine's Day cards and stay faithful. We should put vasopressin in their food.

Testosterone
Without testosterone you can kiss good-bye to an erection. Trust me, I know these things.

Cortisol
I talked about cortisol before; it is your friend and foe. It can get you going, put a tiger in your tank, or debilitate you.

As I mentioned, things are much more complex than I've described because these chemicals affect you in different ways, depending on where in the brain they're switched on. For example, Parkinson's disease patients have too little dopamine in an area of the brain that controls movement. If you increase their dopamine, the shaking stops but now there's too much dopamine in other parts of the brain so you've got a guy who's suddenly addicted to gambling or sex. Now he's not shaking but he's broke and making eyes at you. You see the problem? For depression it's not as simple as increasing your serotonin because if you pump it in, it's like cluster-bombing; what's effective in one area may damage the next. Neuroscientists are still in the dark about antidepressants because how can they research what happens to neurons when there are hundreds of billions of them? (Like finding your contact lens in the Sahara.)

MEMORY

Here's where knowledge of the brain gets fuzzy: around memory. Neuroscientists are unable to identify where memory is located in the brain; it seems it's everywhere. If the amygdala is persistently stimulated or there's a big enough shock, the synapses change shape, making them more sensitive to fear stimuli, and you'll feel fear faster next time something similar happens to scare you. If the motor cortex is stimulated enough by firing neurons in that region you'll learn the skills to whack a tennis ball or ski like an Olympian. Pain is learned through over-stimulated neurons in the somatosensory cortex so, by merely touching something, the sensation is more easily triggered, magnifying the agony. So memory is the result of long-term potentiation causing the neurons to be more readily fired.

Most of the understanding about memory comes from either brain accidents or traumas. There was a guy named H.M. who, when he was nine years old, fell off his bike. He was fine for a while, but by age twenty-five he had started having severe seizures. To find a way to alleviate these episodes, the surgeon took out both the right and left sides of his hippocampus; no one had ever done that. He seemed fine but for a tiny problem:

Whatever he did, he couldn't remember that he had done it before. He'd eat and not know it and eat again. Each time he met someone it was as if it was the first time. (No short-term memory.) If you were a comedian this man would be your ideal audience. It became clear that you need your hippocampus to convert short-term memory into long-term memory. What was amazing was that he could remember everything before the accident, so his long-term memory was intact. Clearly memory is stored in other parts of the brain.

There are two major kinds of memory processes—explicit and implicit.

Explicit Memory

Your explicit memories are stored in the hippocampus and medial temporal cortex and include facts, events, people, and places. You need to make a conscious effort to recall these memories— for example, when was your first kiss and where? For me it was in my closet with God knows who . . . I was stoned. (I hope it was a person and not a shoe.)

Implicit Memory

Implicit memories are unconscious memories: When you learn to ride a bike, you're firing off clusters of neurons that help you pedal and balance, and every detail becomes automatic so you don't have to think back to remember them. Implicit memory is stored in various places in the brain; movement is stored in the motor cortex and cerebellum, and the memory of certain emotions is stored in the amygdala.

For the first eighteen months of our lives we encode only implicit memory: smells, tastes, sounds, bodily, and emotional sensations. The brain combines similar events and constructs mental models from repeated events. If Mommy hugged you repeatedly during childhood, you'd start to expect it whenever you saw her. This information is then embedded in your synaptic connections, which ultimately shape your brain so whenever you see Mommy or someone who looks like her, you're primed to expect that hug. (I find these people particularly irritating, and even worse, they want a hug back. I am going to make a T-shirt that says "No Hugs.")

Your hippocampus pulls together separate images and sensations from implicit memory, like pieces of a puzzle, into pictures of factual and autobiographical material.

In order to couple the details of an experience with an emotional kick, the hippocampus has to work with other limbic areas like the amygdala—this is why you'll never forget the smell of the sea on the night your boyfriend threw you off a cliff.

When images and sensations stay in implicit memory and aren't integrated by the hippocampus they remain disconnected from the past. This could explain the way you have flashbacks from traumatic experiences because you can't identify the fear and panic as belonging to the past.

Autobiographical Memory

As time goes on, you collect and condense more and more episodic memories into larger files along a timeline. At this point you can start to tell funny or sad stories about different times in your life, compare various experiences, and create a narrative. As you elaborate these multiple episodes you eventually have yourself an autobiography; now you can write a book about the story of your life (whether anyone will buy it is a separate question).

How Memory Works

The mind is always recording whether you're awake or asleep. We sometimes dip into our consciousness and maybe pick out a few random words or snippets of thought and embroider them together to form a tale. This random fishing in thoughts does not actually reveal who you are. I apologize to any Freudians reading this but scrutinizing the minutiae of your thoughts is like studying your feces through a microscope. If you learn about yourself from that, good luck to you.

Whenever you use memory, you're retrieving it from storage in the various parts of your brain working together to create the remembered event. It uses the emotional impact—your fear, joy or shame—to color how you'll remember something. The image is imprinted by what you felt. Also, your feelings in a situation will be as different from the next person as your fingerprint. This is why so many people remember the scene of a crime differently. We are all biased in terms of how we bring up the past. Each time a memory is recalled, it is an amalgamation from various sections of the brain. If you call it up again and again you get versions of old versions like an elaborate game of telephone, and each time it becomes more distorted.

Our brains collect images from the moment we're born and file them away as either safe or dangerous. Whenever we see someone or something, we dive into our memories to see who that person or scene reminds us of. In our visual cortex there is a region for face recognition. Its job is comparing who's in front of you with faces you recall from the past. All of this happens in a billionth of a second and is under the radar, so we don't realize how biased our judgment is when we meet a new person, making bigots and sexist pigs of us all. So if I meet a slightly obese, older woman with dyed red hair and wire-rimmed glasses, I will probably be hostile because my grandmother looked like that and always took out her false teeth in front of my friends. This poor woman won't know why I'm treating her like a leper.

The whole brain works as a unit to keep you alive. Isn't that heartwarming? Someone cares. You. Each of these parts of your brain individually wouldn't know what to do and would be just a lump of uselessness but all together they are more complex than the universe and beyond. (See *Star Trek*.)

If, say, you're walking in the jungle and there's a curvy thing on the ground. In the first few tenths of a second light bounces off the curvy thing and is sent to the occipital cortex where it's registered, then for further processing the image is sent to the hippocampus (the filing cabinet) to evaluate if it's a threat or an opportunity. If the hippocampus gets a slight feeling this squiggly thing could be dangerous, it sends out a "jump-now-check-later" message, which informs the amygdala, which in turn rings the alarm, "Emergency, emergency." This warning notifies your fight-or-flight neural and hormonal systems, and at that point your reproductive and digestive organs shut down because, as I've said, the last thing you need to do when you're about to be obliterated is to eat or procreate. Almost immediately, blood and oxygen drain from your brain to shoot into your arms and legs to get you ready for fight or flight. Your heart speeds up, your breathing accelerates. Your memory and any clear thinking are obliterated because all your glucose and blood have left the building and are heading out to your peripheries.

Meanwhile the slow prefrontal cortex has been yanking information out of long-term memory trying to figure out if it's a stick or a snake. It may register that no one else around has panicked and, after a few more seconds, access the neurons it needs to fire into the pattern that informs you it's a stick. How about that for teamwork? Eventually this experience works its way to the language centers but not until much later, so in the height of panic you have no words. It takes about 240 milliseconds for you to even start a grunt. And then let the swearing begin.

How You Developed

Evolution plays its part in creating an experience-dependent brain in that you are born inside out (don't panic, it all works out) so when you're only a one-month-old embryo, your outer layer of cells folds inward, forming your brain stem, and this is why our insides were once literally connected to the outside. The DNA instructs the neurons on which area they should migrate to. They then connect to each other, based on your experience, and that ultimately will determine how your brain is shaped. Only the strong and often-used neurons survive, and the rest die off, like sperm that don't make it through the big swim.

Somehow every single cell has to know if it's a cell for your nose or part of your toenail and find its way to that particular area. No GPS, no nothing. Can you imagine that kind of a challenge? Trillions of cells trying to put together the puzzle of all your parts; what makes you you. It would be like rush hour, squared. What are the chances that you come out vaguely normal and not looking like a Picasso with three breasts coming out of your forehead? I wouldn't bet on the odds. And let's say you form the full complement of limbs and digits and a brain that works; now you depend on your parents (two descendants of a one-celled amoeba) to fill your tiny empty brain with the first spoonfuls of knowledge; teaching you to talk, walk, think, feel, flirt, and freak out. This is why each of us, each generation, has to struggle with this universal quandary: What are we supposed to be doing here?

How Our Brains Grow

Reptiles lay some eggs or just stand and deliver and move on; without sentimentality they walk away to mate again somewhere with anyone who happens to be mounting them at the time while they're munching on some lawn. Then the baby automatically knows how to swim, slither, trot, or fly away. We are born knowing nothing and just lie there in our own mess till someone lifts us out of it and bothers to change our pants. They (animals) need no manual, they just know things. Compared to other primates, humans are born far too early for their brain to be mature. (If we could stay in our mother's womb for the brain to fully develop we'd be in there twenty-four months.) The only reason we come out at nine months is because our heads wouldn't fit through the birth canal if we stayed in there and would end up doing some serious damage to Mommy; she would probably never walk again and sue us for personal injury. You know that scene in *Ben-Hur* where they tie each of a man's legs to an elephant and then scream, "Giddy up?" That's how Mommy would feel.

The genes build the scaffolding of your head in-vitro but once outside Baby has only his basic amphibian brain, just enough to keep his heart and breathing going and that's about all. But it's not all bad news. Evolution can be smart sometimes, and because we come out so undercooked the development of our brain depends on external experience. We have so much to learn once we're out so we need that external stimuli to develop, which is a blessing because it would be impossible to learn shorthand or Ping-Pong while we're inside the womb. This is a very clever idea because no one knows where you're going to be born, and you need different skills depending on the area and culture you plop out into. If you're born in the

Sahara, it would be good to have a structure that would make you proficient in camel straddling or if you're born in New York, it's more helpful if you develop the motor skills to honk and scream at other drivers. We have so much learning to do. (This is called *neural Darwinism*.)

By age three, the baby's brain has formed about a thousand trillion synaptic connections. At that point, the baby has the equipment to speak any language in the world. Its ears, tongue, and mouth are primed for any sound or accent that may be needed depending on where it's born. The sounds around you shape your tongue and palate, so the first sixteen months will determine your accent. If you're German, you will probably make that sound in your throat that sounds like you're about to bring up phlegm.

Before you learn to speak, your brain is like a wad of chewing gum so any language is possible to learn with the perfect accompanying accent, and unless you become an impressionist, you'll be stuck with it. You better learn fast at this point because after the first two months half your neurons drop dead.

The right hemisphere has a higher rate of growth during the first eighteen months, which establishes the basic structures of attachment and emotional regulation. During the second year of life, a growth spurt happens in the left hemisphere. We learn to crawl, then walk, and then there's an explosion of language skills such as saying "poo, poo." The hands and eyes become more connected to visual stimuli and vocabulary develops, so now we can demand things like a rattle on ice with a splash of vermouth. The language areas are activated by about eighteen months after birth and babies begin to develop self-consciousness, recognizing themselves in a mirror. This is the birth of the concept of "I" when you get that feeling that you are you, if you know what I mean.

As Baby matures, neural circuits, guided by the environment, connect. As sensory systems develop, they provide increasingly precise input to shape neural network formation and more and more complex patterns of behavior. Now Baby can draw like Rembrandt. Movements and emotional networks connect with motor systems so you can spit in someone's face because they have pissed you off. Now all the wires of behavior, movement, sensory experience, and emotions connect and feed each other information, like wires in a complex phone system. Right and left hemisphere integration allows us to put feelings into words. This linking up of right and left hemispheres is accomplished through Mommy and Baby eye contact, facial expressions and speaking "goo goo," which is called "motherese." (Some single women use it with their cats.) The baby imitates Mommy and so he or she learns how to put feelings into words. Then when Mommy rocks the baby, her hormones are released, making baby feel safe. A game of peek-a-boo activates the baby's nervous system by the fine art of surprise and leads to cascades of biological processes enhancing Baby's excitement. Peek-a-boo is not just an aimless activity, it is a brain grower. So forget chess and sudoku; just jump out at someone from behind a door—you'll be doing them a big favor, upping their IQ by thousands.

The memory of how Mommy is with Baby influences the

baby's physiology, biology, neurology, and psychology. How the brain grows is affected by how she put you down, held, smiled, ignored, or forgot you; she is the uber-regulator, the big boss of brain development. The neural clusters for social and emotional learning are sculpted by Mommy's attunement with Baby. She grows these neurons in the baby by making direct eye contact with her left eye to Baby's right eye. This is why Mommies usually hold babies in their left arm so this eye contact is made easier. When they gaze into each other's eyes, their hearts, brains, and minds are linking up. These face-to-face interactions increase oxygen consumption and energy. Also, holding the baby in this position means it can hear Mommy's heartbeat. Seeing her loving face looking down on Baby triggers high levels of endogenous opiates so he experiences pleasure in later social interactions by the positive and exciting stimulation from Mommy.

If the mother is too connected, this affects Baby and later he might feel people are encroaching on his space. If, on the other hand, she is too disconnected, he might in later life feel abandoned and become a comedian looking for constant attention. If the mother soothes the terrified baby, he learns to regulate his own fear. The mother's face shows him what is safe and what isn't. If she shows fear or any negative state, the baby internalizes it. If she expresses depression or shows an expressionless face, the baby, not being able to

Babies are built to engage and respond to the world.

think something is wrong with the mother, believes he is the cause and so has a greater chance of having depression or some other mental dysfunction himself, while keeping an idealized image of his caretaker; his survival depends on her. Babies are built to engage and respond to the world. If they don't get a response, they stop engaging with the world and can become emotionally frozen.

The holding and separating that are repeated by mother and child help the baby to self-regulate throughout his life while he learns how to care for himself. When the mother over-holds you can soon see the results; every Jewish boy's first novel is about mothers who never let go.

Neuroplasticity

As I said right at the beginning of this book, it was thought about ten years ago that, gene-wise, you're hardwired from birth; imprisoned by your DNA. But now science has broken that shackle; change is possible well into old age. It was thanks to a scientist named Michael Meaney that the idea of genetic determinism was toppled like the Berlin Wall; here one day, gone the next. His experiments on rats showed that the way a mother treats her babies determines which genes in the offspring's brains are turned on and which are turned off, demonstrating that the genes we're born with are simply nature's opening shot. If maternal behavior changes, the genes change. Fearful baby rats were put with nurturing mother rats and were licked rather than ignored and their actual genetic expression changed, proving we're not held captive by our genes. (I wouldn't have wanted my mother to lick me but perhaps it would have made me more positive and loving. Who am I to say?)

All this applies to humans in that if you inherit genes that give you a more aggressive, depressive, or anxious nature but if your life, especially your early life, exposes you to empathetic people, those negative genes may never be expressed and their makeup altered.

As I lead you into Part 4, I just want to remind you that the brain changes continuously by every sight, sound, taste, touch, thought, and feeling. Experience and learning remodel new circuits (neurogenesis).

> *The brain changes continuously by every sight, sound, taste, touch, thought, and feeling.*

We do know some of our ingredients and what they do, and maybe in years to come we'll be able to carry around some kind of recipe that will allow us to change who we are day by day. We might decide we want to take a tablespoon of oxytocin and dribble in some dopamine to make us feel good about finishing our homework.

But for right now, the practice of mindfulness gives you some of the utensils that help you turn something you burned and destroyed into something that tastes good and feels soothing inside.

ONE LAST THING

Before I move on to Part 4, I just want to bring your attention to how misguided we are in insisting the external world is exactly as we see it. Much of what you see out there is manufactured by your brain, painted in like computer-generated graphics in a movie; only a very small part of the inputs to your occipital lobe comes directly from the external world. The rest comes from internal memory stores and other processes. Think of the area in your visual cortex, a projection room creating what's out there from incoming information. In actuality we see the world in single snapshots, and it is a part of your brain that makes it seem like it's constantly moving. There are about seventy separate areas working to create a cohesive picture of the world; one part contributes color, another movement, another edges, another picks up shapes and another shadows. There is no single part that gets the whole picture. And in completely different zones, the images get a name, or an association or an emotional tag.

Sorry to be the bearer of bad news again; we live in a *virtual reality*. Think of *The Wizard of Oz*—you're being run by the guy behind the curtain. You get clips that randomly come into your consciousness—never the whole film. So while you're getting these fleeting clips to make you feel that's all that's going on, a trillion things without you knowing it are going on right now inside you.

When you wake up in the morning, you remember who you were the day before because of billions of neurons, electrically zapping around the brain, working around the clock to make you believe you have unity and keep you wanting to exist.

Another thing your remarkable brain is doing is keeping your heart beating more than a hundred thousand times per day. That's forty million heartbeats per year, pumping two gallons of blood per minute, through a system of vascular channels about sixty thousand miles in length or twice the circumference of the Earth. Should I go on? (Skip the rest of this if it gets too much.) Just now a hundred thousand chemical reactions took place in every single one of your cells. Multiply those hundred thousand chemical reactions by the seventy to hundred trillion cells that make up you. (I couldn't do that but maybe you can.) So while your body's doing its thing, you could be using your mind to bring you calm and happiness. What a segue to introduce you to mindfulness.

PART FOUR

MINDFULNESS: TAMING YOUR MIND

MY STORY

This study of neuroscience gave me reassurance through discovering that under our scalps we all look pretty much the same. Knowing this, I felt I was part of the human race. What a relief. (Good news for me, bad news for the human race.) But the course at Oxford was not just about the brain; it was also about learning mindfulness. I thought in my case, what with the Wagnerian opera playing 24/7, I'd never be able to find the inner peace as advertised on the label. For a start, how would I sit still when I was a professional hunter of blue-striped cushions? I decided to go along with it only because I discovered that there's just one letter separating medication with meditation so I figured, why not? (I had to go to Oxford for this?)

I probably don't need to mention that I was very, very skeptical about learning something connected to meditation. I thought it was a Buddhist thing where you have to use long meaningless mantras. Also, I was not about to worship some elephant with a thousand arms or a smiling fat man. Before I become involved, I always wanted things to be tangible; things I can see or taste or touch. Also, if someone ever waves a crystal at me, or tries to read my aura, I politely continue the conversation, smiling and nodding my head in agreement, but inside they are dead to me. I might even take their phone number but ultimately I will throw it away.

With mindfulness, it's a misconception that the point is to empty your mind; you need your mind to analyze, memorize, create, and, most important, exist. It can never be empty while you're alive; even in a coma your mind is still chattering away. The trick is to learn to live with the unrelenting soundtrack.

It isn't easy. Mindfulness is like training in a mental boot camp. It is not for the fainthearted because the mind is like a wild animal demanding you obey its every whim. And you've become so used to being the slave, you obey: "Gotta do this, gotta write email, gotta garden, gotta learn judo, gotta row across the Atlantic." The gottas never stop, and we always do as we are told. It's so much easier to go along with what you're used to; certainty is less threatening than uncertainty even if you suffer because of it. Most of us believe that fundamentally we can't change, and that our thoughts define who we are. This is why you hear the expression "It's beyond my control." People often think that their thoughts are fixed and unchangeable, but that is far from the truth.

TAMING YOUR MIND

With mindfulness practice, you eventually tame, calm, and befriend that bucking bronco of a mind, gently taking the reins and steering it where you want. If you whip or treat a horse cruelly it will most likely throw you into the dirt and probably stamp on you for good measure. If you're gentle with it, soothing it, giving it a little stroke, a shard of straw, and lovingly shout whoa, it will eventually calm down. Same with the mind;

if you're self-critical and demanding, not only do you suffer but now you admonish yourself for your suffering with "Why do I feel this way? I shouldn't feel this way. I'm making myself feel this way because I'm such a . . . [fill in the blank but make it nasty]." When the mind gets agitated and negative, if you are patient and gentle with yourself, it eventually settles down, and you experience something we call peace and, at best, happiness. (For those of us who have been the biggest bullies to ourselves for most of our lives, this is a big challenge.)

It's similar to when you have an argument with someone. If you ratchet up the aggression, the conflict continues; if one person begins to show empathy and kindness, it dies down from a gale force to a gust of wind.

When you stand back and just watch your thoughts and feelings, you find yourself less scattered, more anchored, and clearer thinking.

This does not mean you sit there like a lump of tofu; it means that when your mind does what all of our minds do, which is change—change constantly and never stop chattering—you don't fight it but rather understand and accept it for what it is.

When you stand back and just watch your thoughts and feelings, you find yourself less scattered, more anchored, and clearer thinking. Negative thoughts aren't bad in themselves, but when we ruminate and dwell on them we're giving ourselves a double whammy. I'm thinking, "I'm a failure, therefore I must be a failure to think this way." When you feel you're knee-deep

in a negative mood, it's not only the mood that causes the ultimate suffering; it's how you react to it. So not only did an arrow
shoot you, which hurts, you send in another one to punish
yourself for hurting. That second arrow you shoot at yourself
for feeling anxious, stressed, or depressed is by far the most agonizing. Pain exists but suffering is optional. You can't stop the
unhappy mood, but you can stop what happens next. Fear is in
fact never as bad as the fear of fear.

We don't survive without emotions and thoughts. They are
signals to get our needs met. Without them, mama don't eat
or get new shoes. These emotions have evolved to help us do
something about sticky situations we find ourselves in; fear is
triggered by danger lurking, sadness is evoked when something
of value is lost. Disgust is felt when something is rotten. Anger
arises when a goal is blocked. All of these feelings are tempo-
rary, they are there to alert you in order for you to remedy the
problem, quick. When the situation is resolved, the high octane
of any of these emotions defuses. The only reason emotions
stick around is because of our own emotional reactions to them.
The problem isn't the fear or the sadness; it's how our minds
react to those feelings. When we try to get rid of the feelings,
we create tension, which makes the situation much worse.

Sometimes, I get this familiar ache in my heart and a sense
of stabbing emptiness around my rib cage. I don't even know
what brings it on; it's just familiar like a horrible visitor. What
brings me to my knees though, is the even bigger heart hurt
when I recognize this ghastly guest is back again.

MY STORY

Perhaps it was my depression that made it an emergency to practice mindfulness. It's not because I'm holier than thou; it's because I seriously needed some way to distinguish my negative but helpful voices from the ones only Satan could have recorded. The problem with depression is that you don't see it coming. Routinely practicing mindfulness gives me the ability to keep my ear to the ground to pick up early warnings; the pitter-patter of the earth vibrating before a tsunami. I'm sure it's the same for those with physical disabilities; they often do daily exercises for pain control. The routine practices of mindfulness and physical exercise are the most effective ways to a better life, but most of us would do anything to avoid them. This seems to be universal in the human condition; we avoid what's good for us. Don't ask me why.

Mindfulness means intentionally paying attention, in the present moment, in a nonjudgmental way (you don't snap at yourself when you notice you might not be in a good place). Once you stand back, you don't try to make things different; it's not even about relaxation but about witnessing whatever's going on without the usual critical commentary. Rather than run away or repress negative thoughts and feelings, you learn to relate to them from a different angle, experience them through a different lens. It's the effort of trying to change things from what they are that ultimately exhausts us.

Mindfulness is not complicated. It's something we can all do: notice things. Just by standing back and being aware, you immediately gain a new view of your inner and outer world along with internal changes in the brain (which I'll discuss later). By sharpening your focus on what's happening right now, you start to notice that thoughts aren't facts; they're constantly changing patterns. They come and go, transform, disperse, and dissolve. Finally you can experience them, not as something solid or threatening but as ambient background noise. The idea is to relate to thoughts as merely brain events, rather than absolute truths. Your thoughts are not who you are, they're habitual patterns in the mind, nothing more, and as soon as you see them that way, they lose their sting. I think of them as the noise of a radio in another room; I can pay attention, sing along with them if I want and also choose to ignore them. The big idea is: *Thoughts are not your master; they are your servant.*

> *Your thoughts are not who you are.*

THAT OLD MIND KEEPS ON ROLLING ALONG

The mind is always collecting and collating information from the senses, the environment, or other parts of the mind. Regulating the mind is like driving a car and constantly having to shift gears to adjust to ever-changing road conditions. As each gear has a purpose so have these shifts in the mind. The car can be automatic or manual, and the same is true with the mind; you can choose to respond automatically or you can choose to override it. It's impossible for a car to be in two gears at once. Same with the mind; it can't be in two modes at once because they both require the same mental machinery. You're in charge, and mindfulness gives you the skills to disengage and engage when you choose. The two modes of mind, automatic and manual, could be called "doing" and "being" modes. The practice of mindfulness sharpens your focus so you can do something about your mind being constantly distracted and mentally hijacked. You can do something about those voices, hurrah!

DOING MODE

We live in a constant state of wanting. This need for success, which goes back to our caveman days of living in survival mode, is embedded and reinforced in our culture. If we don't reach these self-imposed goals, we may experience a sense of worthlessness. In my opinion this is why so many people overshop. They might feel they have no worth but their clothes do.

Here is another great gift/glitch: our ability to fill the gap between wanting something and figuring out how to get it. That's what makes us a superior species, the fact that we can review past events in order to ensure successful outcomes in the future. Filling that gap between where we are and where we want to be is probably our biggest motivational driver. That's how a star is born. This is how we achieve, create, produce, and hit the deadline; if we didn't have this ability we would still be sea slugs. There is a fine line between actually wanting to accomplish something and just hard-core desire, and that's where the rips and tears of the human fabric might start. When we get something we want badly, the wanting diminishes, which is great news until the next want comes along. This puts us into a constant state of want, need, lust, greed, and most of the seven deadly sins. (See Dopamine.) (Please don't let me tarnish your trophies for those of you who have just won an Academy Award or a medal in the Olympics—well done, really.)

Another tear in the psyche happens when this need to fill the gap switches on and suddenly we want to know things like, "Why aren't I taller, sexier, more successful?" The trouble is the mind can't distinguish between cognitive problem solving and those rhetorical questions. *Why did he dump me? Why don't I get more tweets? I should be happier, more successful, prettier . . .* Each of these questions only leads to another and another, and because there is no ultimate answer, you'll fall back to your old leitmotif: "I can't find a solution so I must be a failure/weak/stupid." (Pick your poison.)

These gaps in knowledge are impossible to fill because there are no answers to such questions, and they can only lead to more questions. This is why so many existentialists went crazy from thinking too much about why we suffer. That cannot be answered, even if you're Sartre and smoke in Parisian cafés with your smirky, beardy friends. All those "if only" or "I should have" lines of thinking end in tears. This is why some of us are dragged through our lives chasing status, goals, and approval. (See Stand-Up Comedians.) That's the glitch in our machinery. We have to fill that gap to find a solution, and so we go into a frenzy of analyzing until we come up with nothing, then we head into the hills of "What's wrong with me, I must be an idiot." Sulking is the problem, not the solution. And the mind will be in such a frenzy of analyzing the past or future that the present is of no use at all on the problem-solving front.

Critical thinking is one of our highest achievements besides eating with a fork, so when we emotionally can't get what we want, we have to think our way toward the resolution, and this is where we crash and burn.

MY STORY

I don't know if I need to mention my permanent residence at the "doing-mode hotel." My daily routine, before I started mindfulness, involved jolting up from bed at six in the morning after terrifying nightmares of things I forgot to do, followed by a seizure of panic about having to buy a snorkel, which I wouldn't need until my next holiday, six months away. But I felt it would be life-threatening if I didn't hunt one down in five minutes. Like the guy in Dr. Strangelove, *my arm would automatically fling out to grab my computer to Google "snorkel" but at the same time I had to check my emails with the same urgency as Obama probably has when checking if*

North Korea has detonated any nuclear bombs. You can imagine this doing mode led to my demise.

Just a note: This obsessive quality to get things done now at the speed of light has also given me success. The problem, as always, is that I couldn't find the off switch, so everything was done at this pace, consistently leading to burnout. This is a warning to all alphas, whether they're male or female.

The lesson is: How you make money can either make you sick or successful—or both. It's up to you. As long as you're aware you are in doing mode, it won't take over your life. Mindfulness means making a mental note of the state you're in, no matter what that state is. It's about noticing, "Oh, my mind is really a mess with thousands of red hot messages soaring around in there." And not with the accompanying, "I did this to myself, I'm a screw-up." Or worse, depending on how punishing you are to yourself.

Automatic Pilot

Another kick in the ass/gift from evolution is our ability to go on automatic pilot. We need it so as not to have to think about every detail it takes to navigate our environment. We clump all the minuscule movements together and do things without having to think about them. This is to conserve energy in our brain so each time we learn an activity, we don't have to think step by step; we don't have to think, "put key in, turn on engine, look in rearview mirror, release brake" or "reach out for fork, bring to mouth, chew, swallow, and so on." Our brains can daisy-chain thousands of actions together and make them feel seamless; the information goes into our unconscious and we can focus on other tasks.

You can do almost anything in your life on automatic pilot; the problem is you'll miss most of your life just going from one automatic activity to the next. It becomes habit forming. You could end up thinking, eating, reading, getting married, and dying in a haze of unawareness. Some people do. What happens is that you live on autopilot and stop noticing what's happening before your eyes, paying no attention to the present moment. If you're continually on automatic pilot, you won't know that your life has turned into a to-do list. Later down the line, even seeing a friend becomes yet another chore. Some handy questions to find out how much time you spend on autopilot:

A. When you sit down to eat, do you find yourself an hour later having no idea what you just put in your mouth?

B. Do you throw a party and then wake up the next morning with no idea what happened and you weren't drunk?

C. Ever get in your car and then have no memory of how you got where you were going, probably leaving a trail of dead people?

D. Ever come back from a holiday and need photos to remember anything?

E. Ever look in the mirror and think, "Where have I been for the last twenty years?"

F. Ever leave your house and realize you forgot to put on your underpants?

There are no correct answers to these questions because they happen to all of us. Except Oprah and the Dalai Lama.

Depressing Thought

Here's a depressing thought. Suppose your life expectancy is ninety and you're thirty now. That means you have approximately sixty years left. Now let's say you're aware of only a minute every three to five days. This might mean you have only about twelve years left in conscious time. I may not have this exactly right but do you see my point? (I hardly do.) What I'm trying to say is that if you were attentive to your life rather than simply getting through it, then even if a doctor told you that you had only six months to live, if you were awake to every minute, it would be longer than if you had a hundred years to live in an unconscious state. Billions of dollars are spent on longevity. If we lived more mindfully, relishing each moment, think of the savings. We could toss away those vitamins, moisturizers, and surgical appliances because it would seem as if we were living forever. (I point the finger at me on the surgical front.)

BEING MODE

Some people may think, "Oh God, what happens if I get stuck in the being mode and I just end up like a houseplant?" Worry not; our default state of mind is that go-get-it state (otherwise no one would ever endeavor to fly first class).

The doing mode gives you the "go get" to fill the gap between wanting and getting, while the being mode has no voice: It's just directly sensing something and being in the eye of the experience. It's not about spacing out or chilling (no idea what it means, other than getting cozy with my ice cubes), but I experience it when I'm scuba diving; being completely present in a state of bliss and at one with the fish.

Everyone has felt something like this at some point: looking at a sunset, stroking your cat, smiling at a seagull, a moment when time stops and you are not so consumed with you. In this mode, the mind isn't flipping between the past and the future; it has nothing to do, nowhere to go, so it can start to settle and slow down from the high-speed chaos, noticing what's going on in front of your eyes at that moment and experiencing thoughts as passing phenomena that arise and disappear. This state of being, whenever you experience something directly without added inner commentary, as hippie as it sounds, is something that is actually natural. You can still accomplish things but you do them without the overbearing, overburning drive. As Lady Macbeth says, "Thou . . . / Art not without ambition, but without / The illness should attend it." (She knew a thing or two about mental health.)

DOING/BEING: WORKING TOGETHER

With mindfulness, you learn to distinguish the two states of doing and being, shifting mental gears and deciding when you want to be in one or the other. Remember, it's like the gears of a car—you cannot be in both manual and automatic at the same time. There may be times you want to let your mind wander (great ideas come out of daydreaming), reminisce about the past, or make plans for the future, but when you want to pay attention you can switch your focus like the beam of a search light. You'll learn through practice to distinguish when one state is useful and when it isn't. You might be happily regurgitating some old images and suddenly hours or days have passed without you realizing you've been locked in and chained down in memory lane. You could go through a whole lifetime in your head dreaming of another life, instead of living your own.

Steve Jobs, the late chief executive of Apple and a meditator, said:

Remembering that I'll be dead soon is the most important tool I've ever encountered to help me make the big choices in life because almost everything—all external expectations, all pride, all fear of embarrassment or failure—these things just fall away in the face of death, leaving only what is truly important.

MY STORY

When my kids were growing up I could rarely slow down, I was in that full-driven doing mode most of the time. I remember one of my kids once trying to get my attention to show me his dead hamster and help him deal with the funeral arrangements. I couldn't pull the phone away I was so consumed with whatever I was shouting about. I tried to pretend I was interested in the hamster situation but I couldn't take that receiver away from my ear. My kids told me they thought I had two phones growing out of each side of my head like earmuffs. Even one Christmas, when I was dressed as Santa, I hid a speaker in my beard; they knew it and have never stopped busting me about it to this day. They keep asking me what they were like at certain ages and how they acted; I have to check videos to come back with an answer. I'm ashamed to say my mind was elsewhere, either thinking or worrying about the work I didn't get or work I did get. I wish I had practiced mindfulness when my kids were small; I'd be able to remember the dead hamster's name and where we put him.

LEARNING ABOUT MINDFULNESS

One way to learn about mindfulness is to visit a mindfulness-trained instructor to do an eight-week course, two hours a session. For me the instruction manual *is* learning these skills, but please don't think I'm a fanatic and this is the only way to see the light. Everyone will have their own way of taming their mind. But whatever path you choose, it has to be something that doesn't involve running away, encouraging denial, repression, or simply drugging yourself to hide from your own thoughts and feelings. It has to teach you to manage your mind; that way happiness lies. If you can focus your attention at will from the driven mind to the present mind, put down this book; you are probably evolved and have no reason to read on. But if you find that, rather than face the noise in your mind, you would do almost anything for distraction—obsessively clean the house, phone everyone you know and even don't know, email the world, get stoned too often, hit the to-do list—keep reading.

The Development of Mindfulness

It all began with Dr. Jon Kabat-Zinn, who in 1979 set up the Stress Reduction Clinic at the University of Massachusetts Medical School. Since then, he and his team have helped more than ten thousand people with a range of conditions: heart disease, cancer, AIDS, chronic pain, headaches, high blood pressure, sleep disorders, anxiety, panic, gastrointestinal problems, and depression. Kabat-Zinn is not a guru in a bedsheet. He is a professor of medicine emeritus and received his PhD in molecular biology from M.I.T. He created a method to use with patients whose pain was too chronic to remedy, those who were given the diagnosis of "You're going to have to live with this."

He came up with a method called mindfulness-based stress reduction, teaching his patients that, by focusing in on their painful sensations rather than distracting themselves, they'd eventually relate differently and notice that pain was not something solid but a continuously changing landscape. By becoming aware of how transitory it is, they would loosen the pain's viselike grip. He found that if you try to ignore the pain, you're probably tensing other parts of the body, therefore creating stress somewhere else.

Physical Pain

So much of pain is reacting to it, wanting it to go away, hating it, and cursing yourself for having it, but if you explore the bare sensations by going right into it you'll notice that the sensations lose their solidity. Pain is the pure physical "ouch," and suffering is the story you give yourself about that ouch. If it becomes unbearable, try to shift your attention to an area where you don't feel pain, and let your mind rest there. This isn't about being a martyr. This is about choosing where to focus your attention.

EXERCISE FOR PHYSICAL PAIN

You can feel this for yourself, even if you don't suffer from chronic pain, by stretching or bending a part of your body to the point of discomfort, but without stretching beyond your limits. If you send your attention right into that specific region of pain, not thinking about it but trying to experience the specific sensations—whether they're burning, throbbing, stabbing, or pulsing—you'll notice that pain isn't solid or constant but rather a series of sensations, sometimes hard, sometimes light, and even sometimes gone altogether. Go on, try it—flex or bend any part of your body to the point where it starts to ache, and see if you can send your focus directly into that region. Remember to be kind to yourself.

MY STORY

When I was having a root canal recently, I tried to deal with the pain by shifting my attention to an area where I wasn't in complete agony. I tried to send my attention to my toenails. That didn't work so I tried to picture myself in the Bahamas. That didn't work either so I attempted to sing to myself to calm myself down. That didn't work either, but I started to see how hilarious it was; me with my mouth wide open singing lullabies to myself accompanied by the drill. I still had the pain but it took a backseat.

MBCT

Mark Williams (my professor), John Teasdale, and Zindel Segal all worked together to apply Kabat-Zinn's theories to emotional pain and called it mindfulness-based cognitive therapy (MBCT). They began their work with those suffering from depression and taught patients, just like Kabat-Zinn did with those suffering from physical pain, not to try to suppress it but to see if they could locate exactly where the sensation of the emotion is in the body. When you focus in, very gently, on the exact location of where you feel anger, fear, stress, or heartbreak, you'll notice those sensations lose their intensity; they're always coming and going, getting deeper and lighter. They're always changing, and change is the only thing in life you can depend on.

EXERCISE: EMOTIONS

Focus in on a predominant feeling and *notice* where an emotion arises in the body and explore (just as with pain) into the core of the feeling, the edges, pulsing, throbbing, or stabbing. *Notice* how eager your mind is to create a story out of a feeling. (The story might not even have anything to do with the feeling. The mind always wants an explanation.) Just stick with the feeling and skip the running commentary.

MY STORY

This just happened to me today. I was asked to take part in a televised charity event (no names). (Behind the laughing showbiz mask beats a heart of gold.) Everyone who's anyone in the entertainment world wants this job. Well, this year I wasn't asked to go to the fly-ridden country; I wasn't asked to go anywhere. I was asked to go on radio and introduce raising money by playing a prank on David Cameron. So I'm in mid-radio plug, when I'm handed notes about how the prank will raise funds and I see I am not the presenter of this event, someone else is. I am there merely to promote the event.

My stomach dropped thirty thousand feet even though I never left the building, as my ego was shot down in flames. Being a professional, I carried on without a flicker of bitterness showing. The interviewer actually asked what I had to do with the event and I smiled graciously and said, "Nothing." OK, here's the point, I'm there to talk about a charity that prevents starvation and fights disease, and I'm caught in a narcissistic, egotistical massacre. Believe me, I was the first to be aware of how despicable my thoughts are. The thoughts of shame and self-loathing bombarded my brain.

It's at moments like this that you really don't want to feel the full brunt of being carpet-bombed by your own thoughts, but here's the bitch. No matter how much you want to try to run from these recriminating thoughts, they're there bubbling away under the surface.

No matter how many decathlons you run, how many shoes you buy or how famous you get, those unresolved, unbearable feelings exist below. Freud was on the mark when he said you have to bring your darkness into the light if you want to free yourself from those deep unconscious emotions.

Just like a virus has to be sweated out, your malignant thoughts and feelings have to surface.

EXERCISE: RAIN

You can use the acronym RAIN when you're dealing with your emotions. It stands for recognition, acceptance, investigation, and nonidentification.

RECOGNITION

Ever feel overwhelmed? You can't think clearly, your head is full of red mist? First, just recognize whatever you can snatch from the melee, such as fear, rage, or sadness. Even identifying an emotion means you're regulating it; you're using your prefrontal cortex to calm the inflamed limbic system.

ACCEPTANCE

All emotions are OK; it's how you think about them that does the damage. Whatever the feeling is, it is just a feeling. You don't have to act on it. Let it pass through because in the next second it changes anyway. Dump the shame and blame. It will never get you anywhere but back in your head.

INVESTIGATION

You send the focus of attention into wherever the emotional pain is in your body. As soon as you tune into body sensation, the story ends. Go inside: Is your chest tightening? Your stomach churning? Your jaw clenched like in *Alien*? If you register nothing, that's fine too.

NONIDENTIFICATION

Nonidentification means stepping away from the emotions and giving them space so you get that "this too shall pass" vibe. With this distancing, you're developing self-regulation, taking the heat off by paradoxically tuning in to the bare sensations rather than the whys and wherefores. You won't immediately snap out of your sadness and skip through fields, but you'll give yourself that pause to take the burn off and reflect in the midst of it all. The more you practice, the faster you get at identifying and exploring your emotions.

EXERCISE: FIVE SECONDS
(STOP AND NOTICE)

SUGGESTIONS

Set the phone to *ting* every few hours and when it tings, *stop and notice* what's going on in your mind and body and then move on—simple.

When you close your computer, *stop and notice* what's going on in your mind and body and then move on.

When you finish or start eating, *stop and notice* what's going on in your mind and body and then move on.

Here are some daily activities you can use for this five-second exercise.

OPTIONS

Brushing your teeth
Taking a shower
Washing the dishes

Taking out the garbage
Doing the laundry
Opening your computer
Peeling carrots (my idea of hell)
Seeing your kids

Got the idea?

Bonus suggestion: Use the five-second pause when you *notice* yourself going into the doing mode—that is, when you get the first hint that you're starting to mindlessly go from one activity to the next to the next—before you find yourself in the endless to-do list syndrome.

EXERCISE: STOP

. . . .

You notice your mind is wandering, ruminating, or not where you want it to be. Don't! Don't! Don't punish yourself! Just STOP.

S stands for STOP whatever you're doing to notice what's going on in your mind and body. Whatever's happening up there, don't do anything about it. Just STOP.

T stands for THINK. If you are reading this book, THINK, were you actually reading? (I won't get mad if you weren't, this is just an exercise.) If you find that you actually weren't reading, what were you thinking about instead?

Examples: "I need tea, coffee, whipped cream, sex, the phone, to send an email, I should have . . . [fill in], I forgot to . . . [fill in], I didn't . . . [fill in]." Were you in the past, future, planning, worrying, daydreaming, having erotic thoughts? (That would be weird.) If you don't know where your mind was, that's OK. Just register a blank.

The fact that you noticed that your mind was not reading is a great accomplishment. You should blow up the balloons, put on the party hats, and congratulate yourself.

If you have been reading all this time and have been aware of not just the words but the sounds around you, the sensation of your breathing and the feel of your body touching whatever you're sitting on, you are an enlightened being. Read on no more, put down this book, and call the Dalai Lama. You are next in line.

O stands for OPTIONS. If you find your mind is somewhere else, put the book down, close your eyes and pick one of your senses. Focus on:

- The sounds around you
- The smells around you
- The feeling of your body on the chair/bed/sofa, whatever you're on
- The feeling of your breath going in and out of your nose/throat/chest/abdomen or all the way in and all the way out

P stands for PROCEED. Go back to reading my book and don't let me find you losing concentration again.

For me this poem by Portia Nelson sums up the benefit of practicing mindfulness.

AUTOBIOGRAPHY IN FIVE SHORT CHAPTERS

I

I walk down the street.
There is a deep hole in the sidewalk.
I fall in.
I am lost . . . I am hopeless.
It isn't my fault.
It takes forever to find a way out.

II

I walk down the same street.
There is a deep hole in the sidewalk.
I pretend I don't see it.
I fall in again.
I can't believe I'm in the same place.
But it isn't my fault.
It still takes a long time to get out.

III

I walk down the same street.
There is a deep hole in the sidewalk.
I see it there.
I still fall in . . . it's a habit . . . but,
My eyes are open.
I know where I am.
It is my fault.
I get out immediately.

IV
I walk down the same street.
There is a deep hole in the sidewalk.
I walk around it.

V
I walk down another street.

ANCHORING

You might find that just to pause is enough, to relish those few seconds when you come out of your busyness and are able to smell the roses or bathe in what it feels like to be present before going back to what you need to do.

The practice of MBCT gives you the tools so that you become your own shrink (big money saver). You learn to observe your own thoughts. But how do you do that without falling into rumination? Because that's how our minds work, always trying to fathom why we have a problem. With mindfulness you learn a technique of focusing on an anchor, which you can return to when the mind gets too agitated or tries to suck you into its never-ending story. This anchor isn't some wand you have to find in fairyland; it's something we all come equipped with: our senses.

The idea is you focus on one of your senses: listening, seeing, tasting, smelling, touching, or breathing, and when your mind wanders, which all minds do, you *notice* where your mind has gone and then, without any criticism, take or escort your focus back to one of the senses. When you give your full attention to any of these, your autopilot switches off, your mind stops ricocheting from past to future because you don't have to think about a sense, you just experience it. If you pay close attention to what you're immediately experiencing, you're right there in the present; the mind-wandering mode switches off. The brain of someone who is totally focused on one point (someone who has practiced mindfulness even for a few days) has lowered amygdala activity (fear button is off) and has a steady heartbeat and normal blood pressure. He is in a state of well-being.

These anchors provide a place to go back to when you notice rumination beginning. So if you want to investigate how your mind works by practicing mindfulness, you can choose to *notice* where your mind went and then return to a safe harbor by focusing on a sense or the breath. And by noticing without reprimanding yourself and having a safe base, you'll see thoughts and feelings as mental phenomena that aren't threatening. You're strengthening your ability to tune into your mind when you need to create, make decisions, problem solve, compare, and so on, and tune out when your thinking becomes harmful or too critical. What you think about is your choice—you're not the victim of what you think.

Which Anchor to Choose?

It's up to you what you want to focus on, but when you've made your choice, the idea is to try to attend to it for a specific amount of time; otherwise you've still got a mind that jumps from thought to thought. Some people choose to focus on their breath because it's always there and its pattern changes, so you never get bored, as you follow your inhaling and exhaling.

When I'm onstage and I start to lose it, there follows a chain of reactions: my body seizes up, heart starts pounding, panic rises, and I get the old theme tune, "I'm going to flop. Everyone hates me." An audience can always feel your fear and for some evolutionary reason turns hostile, howling like animals baying for blood. It must be some primitive instinct that when someone is failing in front of a large group of people, they, as a gaggle, go in for the kill.

From practicing mindfulness, I've learned that to save my skin, as soon as I recognize I'm going into the high-anxiety mode either by a physical signal (dry mouth, beating heart) or an emotional signal (a stabbing in the stomach), I send my attention to my feet, and their contact with the floor. As soon as my focus goes from thoughts to a sensation, the red mist drains from my brain and I can think again. And when I'm calm and in control, the audience gets calm. It doesn't have to be attention to your feet; using any of your senses will do the trick.

Anchor Options

All of the following anchors take the focus from the busy mind to the experience of a sense, which is always immediate. (You can't hear, taste, touch, or smell something in the past or future, only right now.)

Staying focused without force strengthens the part of the brain that allows you to switch focus when you want to move from the doing mind to the being mind.

You're learning to experience without judgment, treating thoughts and feelings as mental events without identifying with them.

You're learning to be aware of what is there without trying to change or fix things.

By focusing on sight, sound, taste, and touch you're learning that everything takes shape and then dissolves.

You're learning to move focus more adeptly from one area to another and also from a narrow focus; the touch of your foot on the ground to a wide focus; a sense of the whole body from head to toe.

Everyone's mind constantly grabs for attention: If you need to do this a hundred times, then do it a hundred times, just like you did the first time. And this is taming your mind.

EXERCISE: FOCUS ON YOUR FEET

Stand or sit on a chair with your feet on the floor, with your spine straight but not rigid; your eyes can be open or shut (I shut mine, but if you want to keep your eyes open then simply lower your gaze). Now send your attention to the feel of your feet on the ground. *Notice* the precise sensations, the weight, temperature, tingling, or nothing at all. *Notice* when your mind takes over with its commentary and as soon as it does, note where it took you (without judgment) and bring your focus back to your feet. Sounds simple? Try it. How long before your mind grabs you back?

EXERCISE: TASTE

. . . .

Place a piece of chocolate in your mouth. (Now you can get the percentage of actual cocoa in the chocolate. What were we eating before? Paper?) If chocolate isn't your thing, you can choose anything else, as long as it's something you'd put in your mouth and swallow. (Use discretion please—nothing weird.)

Slowly put it on your tongue. *Notice* when your mind has snatched the attention back and where it's taken you and then gently take your focus back to the chocolate. Feel the weight and texture. Is it sweet? Is it salty? *Notice* the sensation of bit-ing, chewing, and swallowing.

Think of your mouth as a laboratory and your tongue your workbench to explore taste. In the past, how many times have you thrown a chocolate in your mouth but your mind was somewhere else? You maybe swooned with the first bite but after a few more chews your mind takes flight to another town. You might even have tasted the first and last bite but were asleep for the bites in between. You paid for the whole chocolate but missed most of the action, not to men-tion, with the enormous calorie intake, you've fattened up your thighs without any epicurean benefit.

EXERCISE: FOCUS ON YOUR SEAT

. . . .

Wherever you're sitting and whatever you're sitting on, *notice* the feeling of the back of your thighs, pelvis or whatever is touching the chair. *Notice* when your mind pulls you away, and move your focus back to your seat on the seat.

EXERCISE: LISTENING TO SOUND

Bring your attention to all the sound around you and tune in like it's your favorite record. Pick up sounds in front, behind, above, and below and the silences in between the sounds. As soon as you *notice* that your mind wandered, take the focus back to the sound.

EXERCISE: BREATHING

Many people use breathing as a point of focus because it gives you a direct insight into your emotional state; noticing the speed and quality (shallow or harsh) of your breath gives you a way to detect your own internal weather patterns. It makes a great anchor because when you notice your mind has wandered, your breath is always there. You don't have to go hunting for it; the breath is always breathing.

Following your breath, it's best to stay with one area either through your nose, throat, chest, or abdomen so your mind stays focused. *Notice* how your breath changes with each inhale and exhale—whether it's light, heavy, short, or long, just noticing that it's always changing and dissolving.

EXERCISE: SMELLING

Smell a lemon/coffee/bread/a baby's head . . . where you stick your nose is up to you. *Notice* every subtlety of the scent, and when your mind takes you away, *notice* where it's gone and come back to the smell.

EXERCISE: TOUCH

. . . .

You don't need to be in any special place to experience mindfulness. It's just about being awake to sensation. You can simply pet your cat/dog/husband . . . your choice. *Notice* the feel of the fur/hair and if your mind takes over, *notice* where it's been and come back to the feeling of petting your pet/husband. (They might be the same thing.)

THE TROUBLE WITH THINKING

. . . .

Thinking becomes a problem when we confuse the thoughts about things with the things themselves. We can think about an imaginary frog in our mind and know it's not the same as a real frog. But when your mind brings up something that physically doesn't exist, such as our self-esteem, it's often hard to see the distinction. Thoughts about our self-esteem are no more real than an imaginary frog. If we switch to the being mode we can see this much more clearly. We can stand back and witness our thoughts and feelings as experiences that come and go in our mind just like sounds, tastes, and sights. So when a thought comes up—"I feel like a failure"—we don't have to take it as a reality and fall into the inevitable rumination. (It's just an imaginary frog.)

EXERCISE: EXPERIENCING
THINKING ITSELF

. . . .

Just as with sounds, *notice* your thoughts as events in the mind, as noise rather than trying to follow the meaning. Some people imagine their thoughts are like clouds in the sky; some are heavy, some light, some threatening but they all keep moving and changing. You can choose whether to jump on one of them but it would be like jumping on a cloud. They aren't solid structures so you'll fall through.

Another metaphor is to imagine your thoughts on a movie screen and you're watching from the audience. *Notice* when you find yourself in the film, among the characters caught up in the plot. As soon as you've noticed without judgment, walk back to your seat and watch the film again. The idea is to see how you get caught, step back, and then reengage. This is called *untangled perception*.

EXERCISE: MOVING

A very portable way of bringing awareness into your daily life is mindfully walking. (You really can't get more portable than this.) You're not trying to get anywhere; you're just noticing each step at a time. *Notice* exactly how you experience your walk, how automatically one foot lifts while the other touches the ground. *Notice* the muscles working inside your legs and what happens to your balance. *Notice* your weight on the ground. *Notice* how quickly your mind kicks in because we rarely just walk; we're usually moving our thinking minds around and our legs happen to be moving. As soon as you *notice* you're lost in thought or making judgments on how you move, bring the focus back to the movement.

Your body is always with you; it's your most accessible anchor. Just be *in* your body as you move, reach, grab, scratch, run. All you have to do is keep bringing your attention back again and again to your body, bringing you right into the moment.

EXERCISE: WIDENING THE FOCUS

You can stay focused on a specific sense in your body, or you can choose to open up your lens of awareness to every sense, all at once, from your head to your toes.

BEING MINDFUL WITH STRESS

Our reactions to stress are automatic, and we are loaded up to the brim with it, from simply getting a plumber to worrying about some ice cap out there somewhere defrosting. Thanks to our ever-speedier culture, most of our lives are now lived in a state of hyperarousal, and almost everything out there seems scary. We're in a constant downpour of adrenaline and cortisol, muscle tension, high blood pressure, and lack of oxygen to the brain—all of which can make us very, very ill. *Notice* when you feel the beginning of stress; closely explore where it is in your body, the size, the edges, the sensations. *Notice* how your breathing and your posture change. *Notice* if your mind starts to kick in with suggestions to get coffee, cigarettes, or tranquilizers. You don't have to suppress the thoughts or the feelings of fear, anger, or hurt but recognize that they are the dandruff of a flaky mind.

> *Each time we face our feelings head-on rather than run, we're building muscle just like any athlete practicing his skills.*

Each time you bring in awareness without trying to change anything, you'll start to see those things that "pushed your buttons" in the past as familiar themes and start to treat them like old friends you don't really like but have learned to put up with. I have a girlfriend who never shuts up, with a voice like a buzz saw. I have learned to love her, even though I can stand her for only ten minutes at a time.

Only with the regular exercise of bringing awareness to negative thoughts and feelings will you be able to break those mental and physical habits. If you learn to ground yourself in your body, your breath, or in one of your senses, you'll dampen the anxiety, fear, or depression as it's coming down the pipeline so that you can rebalance more quickly. You have lots of opportunities to practice on your stress and you'll fail many times, but just by altering your attention, you're creating new patterns of behavior. Each time we face our feelings head-on rather than run, we're building muscle just like any athlete practicing his skills.

Acceptance isn't resignation. You don't just lie back in your sombrero saying mañana. It provides you with a means of responding skillfully rather than the usual knee-jerk reaction.

The great thing about all these exercises is they're portable so you can use them anywhere, anytime, in any position. Also it's cheap (because it's free).

LAST BUT NOT LEAST: KINDNESS

When you turn your attention in and listen to your own personal dictator, chances are you'll punish yourself. Knowing that the enemy is not without but within is enough to make you self-flagellate for years. The harder you are on yourself, the louder the critical voice gets. Judging and evaluating are cousins to rumination and the "doing" mode. When we make any sort of judgment we're comparing how we want things to be to how they are and trying to fill that gap. The habit of judging ourselves is what pounds us into the ground.

You're being kind to yourself by intentionally moving your attention from the mind to the body. Your body can withstand emotions; your mind can't because it is hardwired to come up with a solution when there isn't one. Think of the body as a safe harbor when you're being ravaged by the "Slings and arrows of outrageous fortune." This is spoken by Hamlet, a man who could have used a class in mindfulness. (He went nuts from overpondering.)

> *The habit of judging ourselves is what pounds us into the ground.*

If a friend was being abused you wouldn't shout at her to stop suffering; you would soothe her pain. So when you're possessed by the demons of your own making, you should treat yourself like you would that friend. The main thing that calms your mind is compassion for yourself. I know that idea makes many people wince (it has the whiff of patchouli oil), thinking they're being self-indulgent, but being kind to yourself when you notice your mind has wandered calms down the vicious thought patterns, which in turn impacts the rewiring of neurons.

Another poem that sums up my experience with mindfulness is this one by Rumi:

THE GUEST HOUSE

This being human is a guest house.
Every morning a new arrival.

A joy, a depression, a meanness,
some momentary awareness comes
as an unexpected visitor.

Welcome and entertain them all!
Even if they're a crowd of sorrows,
who violently sweep your house
empty of its furniture,
still treat each guest honorably.
He may be cleaning you out
for some new delight.

The dark thought, the shame, the malice,
meet them at the door laughing, and invite them in.

Be grateful for whoever comes.
because each has been sent
as a guide from beyond.

Kindness to Others

Not only is compassion good for our health but the impact of the hormones we produce in ourselves pass from person to person. We can pass on our neuroses, but we can also pass on our feelings of warmth and kindness. You get a sudden rush of oxytocin, which makes you feel safe and soothed and therefore switches it on in others around you. We are social animals not made for isolation so all our feelings ripple out to the next person, working like *neural Wi-Fi* (the emotional game of hot potato again). When you're calm and at ease, you have the free space in your head to listen to someone else, to be curious about his life so that he feels he matters. When you get into the habit of passing warmth, humor, and compassion, I'd say you might just experience what happiness feels like. (To me, it feels like someone is tickling my heart.) If you pass on these qualities and the other person lights up with happiness, it comes right back at you.

FACTS ABOUT MINDFULNESS

The real reason I began to practice mindfulness seriously was because of the empirical evidence of what happens in the brain.

It wasn't good enough that mindfulness helped me deal with the depression or that it brought me calm in the storm; ever the skeptic, I demanded hardcore proof. It appeared I didn't trust my own feelings as much as I did science. There are so many data to show the practice doesn't just ameliorate physical and emotional pain. It sharpens your concentration and focus and therefore gives you the edge when others are floundering in the mud. (If that's what you're after.)

Here is just some of the evidence that swung the jury in favor of mindfulness (for me).

Connection to Feelings

A number of studies have found mindfulness results in increased blood flow to the insula and an increased volume and density of gray matter. This is a crucial area of the brain that gives you the ability to focus into your body and connects you to your feelings, such as butterflies in your stomach, or a blow to the heart. Strengthening your insula enhances introspection, which is the key to mindfulness.

Self-Control

Researchers found that increased blood flow to the anterior cingulate cortex after just *six thirty-minute meditation sessions* strengthened connections to this area, which is crucial for controlling impulse, and may help explain why mindfulness is effective in helping curb addictions and other forms of self-control.

Counteracting High Anxiety

Researchers from Stanford found that after an eight-week mindfulness course, participants had less reactivity in their amygdala and reported feeling fewer negative emotions.

Quieting the Mind

The brain stem produces neurotransmitters that regulate attention, mood, and sleep. These changes may explain why meditators perform better on tests of attention, are less likely to suffer from anxiety and depression, and often have improved sleep patterns.

Regulating Emotions

The hippocampus is involved in learning and memory and can help with reactivity to stress. Increased density of neurons in this area may help explain why meditators are more emotionally stable and less anxious.

Regulating Thoughts and Emotions

Changes in the cerebellum are likely to contribute to meditators' increased ability to respond to life events in a positive way.

Curbing Addictive Behavior

The prefrontal cortex is involved with self-regulation and decision making. Mindfulness has been found to increase blood flow to this area, which enhances self-awareness and self-control, helping you to make constructive choices and let go of harmful ones.

Curbing OCD

PET scans were performed on eighteen patients with OCD before and after ten weeks of mindfulness practice. None took medication and all had moderate to severe symptoms. PET scans after treatment showed activity in the orbital frontal cortex had fallen dramatically, meaning the worry circuit was unwired. It was the first study to show that mindfulness-based cognitive therapy has the power to systematically change brain chemistry in a well-identified brain circuit. Intentionally making a mindful effort can alter brain function, and this induces neuroplasticity. This is the first time it was established that mindfulness is a form of experience that promotes neuroplasticity.

A Quicker Brain

Researchers from the University of California, Los Angeles (UCLA) have found that meditators have stronger connections between different areas in the brain. This greater connectivity is not limited to specific regions but is found across the brain at large. This greater connectivity increases the ability to rapidly relay information from one area to the next, giving you a quicker and more agile brain.

Training Your Brain (As Well as Your Body)

A trained mind is physically different from an untrained mind. You can retain inner strength even though the world around you is frantic and chaotic. People are trying to find the antidotes to suffering so it's time we start doing the obvious: training our brains as we do our bodies. Changing the way you think changes the chemicals in your brain. For example, the less you work out, the lower the level of acetylcholine, and the less you have of this chemical, the poorer your ability to pay attention. Even with age-related losses, almost every physical aspect of the brain can recover and new neurons can bloom.

More Positive Research on Mindfulness

- Research from Harvard University suggests that we spend nearly 50 percent of our day mind-wandering, typically lost in negative thoughts about what might happen or has already happened to us. There is a mind-wandering network in the brain, which generates thoughts centered on "me" and is focused in an area called the medial prefrontal cortex. Research has shown that when we practice mindfulness, activity in this me center decreases. Furthermore, it has been shown that when experienced practitioners' minds do wander, monitoring areas, such as the lateral prefrontal cortex, become active to keep an eye on where the mind is going and if necessary bring attention back to the present, which results in less worrying and more living.

- Researchers from the University of Montreal investigated the differences in how meditators and nonmeditators experience pain and how this relates to brain structure. They found that the more experienced the meditators were, the thicker their anterior cingulate cortex and the lower their sensitivity to pain.

- Researchers from Emory University found that the decline in cognitive abilities that typically occurs as we age, such as slower reaction times and speed of thinking, was not found in elderly meditators. Using fMRI, they also established that the physical thinning of gray matter that usually comes with aging had actually been remarkably diminished.

- Researchers from UCLA found that when people become aware of their anger and label it as "anger," the part of the brain that generates negative emotions, the amygdala, calms down. It's almost as if once the emotional message has been delivered to the conscious mind it can quiet down a little.

- Mindfulness activates the "rest and digest" part of our nervous system and increases blood flow to parts of our brains that help us regulate our emotions, such as the hippocampus, anterior cingulate cortex, and the lateral parts of the prefrontal cortex. Our heart rate slows, our respiration slows, and our blood pressure drops. A researcher from Harvard called the changes in the body that meditation evokes the "relaxation response"—basically the opposite of the stress response. While the stress response is extremely detrimental to the body, the relaxation response is extremely salutary and is probably at the root of the wide-ranging benefits mindfulness has been found to have, both mentally and physically.

Mindfulness and the Body

- Researchers from the University of Wisconsin Madison investigated the effects of mindfulness on immune system response. They injected participants with a flu virus at the end of an eight-week course and found that the mindfulness group had a significantly stronger immune system compared with the others.

- Scientists at UCLA found mindfulness to be extremely effective at maintaining the immune system of HIV patients. Over an eight-week period, the group that wasn't taught mindfulness had a 25 percent fall in their CD4 cells (the "brains" of the immune system), whereas the group that was taught mindfulness maintained its levels.

- Researchers from the University of California, Davis, found that improved psychological well-being fos-

tered by meditation may reduce cellular aging. People
who live to more than a hundred have been found to
have more active telomerase, an enzyme involved in
cell replication. The researchers found that the meditators had a 30 percent increase in this enzyme linked
to longevity following a three-month retreat.

- Skin disorders are a common symptom of stress. The
University of Massachusetts gave mindfulness training to psoriasis sufferers and found their skin problems
cleared four times faster than those who weren't
taught the technique.

- Researchers from the University of North Carolina
have found mindfulness to be an effective method
of treating irritable bowel syndrome (IBS). Over a
period of eight weeks, participants either were taught
mindfulness or went to a support group. Three months
later, they found that on a standard five-hundred-
point IBS symptom questionnaire, the support group's
score had dropped by thirty points. The mindfulness
group's score had fallen by more than a hundred
points.

- Researchers from Emory University investigated
whether training in compassion meditation could reduce physiological responses to stress. Participants
were stressed by being requested to perform a public-
speaking task. The researchers found that the participants who had practiced the most had the lowest
physiological responses to stress, as measured by re-

duced pro-inflammatory cytokines and also reported the lowest levels of psychological distress.

• Researchers investigated the physiological effects of an eight-week mindfulness program on patients suffering from breast cancer and prostate cancer. In addition to the patients reporting reduced stress, they found significant reductions in physiological markers of stress, such as reduced cortisol levels, pro-inflammatory cytokines, heart rate, and systolic blood pleasure. A follow-up study a year later found these improvements had been maintained or enhanced further.

Mindfulness and Emotions

• Researchers from the University of Massachusetts Medical School investigated the effects of an eight-week mindfulness course on generalized anxiety disorder. Ninety percent of those taught the technique reported significant reductions in anxiety.

• Studies from the University of Wisconsin suggest that meditators' calmness is not a result of becoming emotionally numb—in fact they may be able to experience emotions more fully. If asked to enter into a state of compassion, then played an emotionally evocative sound, such as a woman screaming, they showed increased activity in the emotional areas of the brain compared to novices. However, if asked to enter into a state of deep concentration, they showed reduced activity in the emotional areas of the brain compared with novices. The key is that they were better able to control their emotional reactions, depending on the mental state they chose to be in.

- Optimists and resilient people have been found to have more activity in the front of their brains (prefrontal cortex) on the left-hand side, whereas those more prone to rumination and anxiety have more on the right. Researchers from the University of Wisconsin found that after eight weeks of mindfulness practice, participants had been able to change their baseline levels of activity moving more toward left-hand activation. This suggests that mindfulness can help us change our baseline levels of happiness and optimism.

- If you suffer from recurring depression, scientists suggest that mindfulness might be a way to keep you free from it. Researchers from Toronto and Exeter in the UK recently found that learning mindfulness, while tapering off antidepressants, was as effective as remaining on medication.

- Researchers from Stanford University have found that mindfulness can help with social anxiety by reducing reactivity in the amygdala, an area of the brain that is typically overactive in those with anxiety problems.

- Researchers at the University of Manchester tested meditators' responses to pain, by heating their skin with a laser. They found that the more meditation the subject had done, the less they experienced pain. They also found that they had less neural activity in the anticipation of pain than controls, which is likely to be due to their increased ability to remain in the present rather than worry about the future.

- A recent study from Wake Forest University found that just four twenty-minute sessions of mindfulness training a day reduced pain sensitivity by 57 percent—an even greater reduction than drugs such as morphine.

- Numerous studies have found that mindfulness on its own or in combination with medication can be effective in dealing with addictive behaviors, from drug abuse to binge eating. Recently researchers from Yale School of Medicine found that mindfulness training of less than twenty minutes per day was more effective at helping smokers quit than the American Lung Association's gold standard treatment. Over a period of four weeks, on average, there was a 90 percent reduction in the number of cigarettes smoked from eighteen per day to two per day, with 35 percent of smokers quitting completely. When they checked four months later, more than 30 percent had maintained abstinence.

- Researchers investigated the impact of mindfulness on the psychological health of ninety cancer patients. After seven weeks of daily practice, the patients reported a 65 percent reduction in mood disturbances including depression, anxiety, anger, and confusion. They also reported a 31 percent reduction in symptoms of stress and less stress-related heart and stomach pain.

- Researchers from the University of California, San Diego, investigated the impact of a four-week mindfulness program on the psychological well-being of students, in comparison to a body-relaxation technique. They found that both techniques reduced distress, but mindfulness was more effective at developing positive states of mind and at reducing distractive and ruminative thoughts. This research suggests that mindfulness training delivers benefits over and above simple relaxation.

Mindfulness and Thoughts/Cognition

- Researchers from Wake Forest University investigated how four twenty-minute sessions of mindfulness practice could affect critical cognitive abilities. They found that the mindfulness practitioners were significantly better than the control group at maintaining their attention and performed especially well at stressful tasks under time pressure. (This is another study demonstrating that significant benefits can be enjoyed from relatively little practice.)
- Researchers from the University of Pennsylvania wanted to investigate how mindfulness could help

improve thinking in the face of stress. So they taught it to U.S. marines before their deployment to Iraq. In cognitive tests, they found that the marines who practiced for more than ten minutes a day managed to maintain their mental abilities in spite of a stressful deployment period, whereas the control group and those practicing less than ten minutes could not.

- Researchers from UCLA conducted a pilot to investigate the effectiveness of an eight-week mindfulness course for adults and adolescents with ADHD. More than 75 percent of the participants reported a reduction in their total ADHD symptoms, with about a third reporting clinically significant reductions in their symptoms of more than 30 percent.

- Researchers conducted a pilot study to investigate the efficacy of mindfulness in treating OCD. About 60 percent of the participants experienced clinically significant reductions in their symptoms, of more than 30 percent. The researchers suggest that the increased ability to let go of thoughts and feelings helps stop the negative rumination process that is so prevalent in those suffering from OCD.

I hope these facts have not put you to sleep because for me these research findings make me feel I'm in well-researched hands. If it's good enough for Harvard, UCLA, the University of Pennsylvania, Yale School of Medicine, and Stanford, it's good enough for me.

MY OWN PERSONAL
RESEARCH FINDINGS

I've been practicing and studying mindfulness for quite a while now. It's helped me decrease the volume of the voices, defuse the onslaughts of self-recrimination, and control my rage at others. Ten or twenty years ago, I imagined that I would be very depressed to say the least when I got to this age but I am happier or at least more content than I have ever been before. Here's how my life has changed so far.

Miracle 1

I have not passed the recordings of self-abuse to my children. I married my husband for his genes; he is that English type whose relatives not only survived the Blitz but they had a "bloody jolly time" in it and still talk of the experience with fondness. Unlike me, my kids are not consumed by envy. Both daughters have friends who are already successful or getting prestigious jobs, and guess what their reaction is? They are happy for them. They make collages with photos of their happy moments together; they are overjoyed for their friends. A miracle. When anyone ever got in my way when I was a child (which was pretty much everyone) I made plans to cut them open and remove their hearts.

Miracle 2

I am not, as my father predicted, a heroin addict by age fifty. He would not listen to me when I said that people who shoot heroin usually start earlier, because he knew better. By fifty, I would be a bum and shooting heroin. So the miracle is that, against all his clairvoyant predictions, I'm not howling like a werewolf to the winds like my mother, and though I have depression, I have built a verbal castle wall around myself. My mantra is "I have an illness. I am not stupid, crazy, brain-damaged, slow, a failure, a moron. I simply have an illness."

Miracle 4
(I Missed 3 Because I Have Dyslexia)

I got into the Royal Shakespeare Company. No explanation. I was not very talented but had the drive of a Rottweiler.

Miracle 5

I got into Oxford and completed my master's degree. (See Miracle 4.)

Miracle 6

Before the last egg left the building and against all odds, I got not one but three "normalish" children.

Miracle 7

My daughters are the prom queens I always wanted to be; everyone returns their calls, they are invited to every party, they are surrounded by friends who love them, they are not eaten up by ambition, and they do not know what it feels like to be left out.

Miracle 8

I did a TED Talks Global. I shat in my pants, but I did it.

Miracle 9

I am writing a book and by this time hopefully have finished it or you're looking at blank pages.

Miracle 10

I had a pretty good career in entertainment until the breakdown.

So, HAHAHAHAHAHAHAHAHA to all my teachers who gave me D's in high school. HAHAHAHAHAHAHA to my parents who claimed I was slightly retarded. HAHAHAHAHA to all the people who tortured me in the playground.

(Sorry if this appears too narcissistic but I still carry some of that particular juice.)

PART FIVE

ALTERNATIVE
SUGGESTIONS FOR
PEACE OF MIND

THE MANUAL

try to practice some type of mindfulness for around twenty minutes when I get up each morning, as well as for five to ten minutes when I notice I'm tipping toward destructive thinking, along with a lot of five-second bursts when I just want to stand back and notice what's going on. I use it now when in the past I would have popped a Xanax. It's an ongoing process, not a magic bullet, but I would call myself at this point "a recovered ruminator." I still wake up with the impulse to leap upright from my bed with my demented to-do list—for example, with the compulsion to return a candle I bought six years ago. Nowadays the internal commands are less burning, and I don't always obey them. I still think about the candle but won't necessarily hunt through my receipts to prove I bought it. We have no bouncer at the doors of our mind to discriminate what gets into our consciousness and what doesn't, so some days it's like an overcrowded disco in my brain and I just have to sit it out, letting it "party on" while underneath trying to track the feel of my breath. If I can sense even one complete inhale or exhale, I've accomplished a great feat.

If I didn't have mindfulness, I would never stop the emailing until death do us part. For me mindfulness works; for others it might not. I don't like yoga; friends of mine adore it (especially Bikram where you boil your bones to bend them). I would rather shoot myself than jog (I've ground my knees down to my ankles trying to do it); others can't live without it. Many people have their particular thing that helps them cope with the ongoing battle in their brains, so who am I to say what would work for them?

WE ALL NEED AN ANCHOR WE CAN LEAN ON

If mindfulness isn't for you, I'm going to suggest some alternative practices to help you deal with everything from life's little hiccups to the gale force ten, brain-shattering breakdowns.

The important thing is that you find something to anchor you when the winds of "shit happens" get rough. So many people I know don't have an antidote for life's turbulent weather and suffer because of it. They ask me, "Should I leave my husband? Change jobs? Stop eating cheese? Take up alcoholism?" Why, if we're still breathing and eating, is there such unhappiness? Dissatisfaction is part of the deal of living because simple existence is full of contradictions; we want individuality, to stand out from the crowd, yet we want to be part of a tribe. We're driven and busy and yet we want peace. And worst of all, we want things to stay the same despite the fact that everything changes (that's the ultimate bummer). Why, oh, why can't we remain young or stay in love forever? We can't. Impermanence is the law of the universe—no can do. Even if you rage through the night, before you finish reading this sentence, billions of your cells have died and been reborn. Because we have consciousness, we suffer about the fact that we suffer, and this second arrow of suffering is constructed in our brains. But if our brain can create this pain, it can also create happiness.

The skill required to tame your mind is to be able to inhibit your attention on certain things and intentionally take your focus to others. This is self-regulation, becoming the captain of the ship, steering your attention where you want it to be. An expert at self-regulation would be able to stay calm even in the face of my mother during one of her episodes.

When you find your particular practice, you'll have found not only *the manual* but also your ticket to your version of happiness.

WHY LEARNING TO PAY ATTENTION IS IMPORTANT

Attention is like a spotlight and what it illuminates streams into your mind, so developing control over it is the most powerful way to shape your brain.

I can hear you say, "What's with attention? I use it when I cross the street." No, for most of us, we are there physically but our attention could be in Sri Lanka. There is a big difference between experiencing something and being aware. The word *experience* comes from the Latin *experiri*, meaning "to try." The word *awareness* comes from the Greek *horan*, which means "to see." (I looked this up—I don't automatically know these things.) Experience is just showing up even though your mind is elsewhere; awareness is when you notice you're there.

We don't naturally pay attention; we have to learn it. (See Glitch in Evolutionary Development.) The tragedy of most of our lives is that we're asleep at the wheel and no one tells us how to wake up. They say to kids at school, "Pay attention." How would they know how to do that? No one teaches them.

Scientists now have the technology to be able to trace what people's eyes focus on when they scan a room. Who or what an individual seeks out is based on genes, chemicals, culture, relationships, and experience. What your eyes fasten onto is where your mind is in any one moment. Some people enter a room and zoom in on a daddy figure (nice but not sexy) or a sugar daddy (same, but with expensive shoes).

We become the character we are at any particular moment depending on what we focus on. On the golf course, swinging the club, you're a sportswoman. In bed in your nightie, you might be a sex kitten. With your kids you may be Mother Goose. (God help you if you ever get these roles confused.) These identities are all transitory; they come and go depending on which metaphorical clothes you wear and for what occasion.

You are where your attention is at any moment. An fMRI scanner can pick up the different neuronal patterns created when you focus on different objects, and their patterns reflect how and what you think.

We're living in a society that encourages multitasking; all interruptions by phones, texts, emails, or other "luminous rectangles" are welcome and, what's more, make us feel warm and wanted. "I'm busy, therefore I am." (A slight twist on the Descartes line.) Brain research shows that rather than it being a great accomplishment of humankind to be able to juggle

> *You are where your attention is at any moment.*

everything, it may actually scramble your brain. (Duh!) The part of the brain you need for learning and memory, the hippocampus, is active during uninterrupted focus. Interruptions of attention impair learning, so if you're trying to learn Mandarin while speed walking on a treadmill, forget about it; it won't stick. You need focused attention to grow neural connections in the hippocampus; that's how learning happens. Focused attention builds up gray matter in the brain, which increases the ability to remember, attend, inhibit, and execute actions, no matter what age you are.

Another reason attention is the road to freedom is that it allows you to see things as if for the first time, and novelty is a component of happiness. If you actually taste, smell, or touch something as if for the first time, you feel alive, excited, and rediscover that sense of wonderment you had as a child when everything gave you a buzz. If you see the world through curiosity rather than a seen-it, done-it lens, you'll notice things you never noticed before, even if you've driven down the same road a thousand times. When you experience novelty, neurogenesis takes place (more neurons connect and make thicker clusters of information). I know that if it were easy to pay attention, we'd all be able to snap out of our reverie at will. We'd all be able to intentionally smell the roses, which is an expression I find very irritating because who has time to do that?

The reason we don't visit the present too often is because evolution dictated that if we spent too much time in the moment, our survival would be in jeopardy. What if you're smelling the roses and some predator comes up behind you? You'd be, like, "so dead." This constant trawling the past to make sure we have a future is what keeps us alive. Awareness in the present can be only fleeting; maybe that's the beauty of it. Eventually your mind will always drag you where it needs to be, scanning the horizon with seemingly disconnected, inconsequential streams of consciousness. This is our tragedy. You might be in the midst of watching the opening ceremony of the Olympics, jaw on the floor and still your mind will drag you back to, "Why didn't my mother let me get a real Christmas tree? My bra had those foam cups in it, where did I leave them? I will never forgive Dagmar Stuart for stealing my Barbie doll's cocktail dress. I have to buy shampoo, I hate my feet, is it too late to take up pole vaulting?" This cacophony of senseless banality is our destiny, our curse. But you can break this circuit; when you begin to train your attention; unwiring old patterns and rewiring new ones, you promote *neuroplasticity*. Whatever you practice, you have to train regularly; only with repetition can you unwire the old habits and rewire the new.

COGNITIVE BEHAVIORAL THERAPY (CBT)

Cognitive behavioral therapy was originally conceived by Dr. Aaron T. Beck, who began in the mid-1950s giving patients a means to observe their thoughts and beliefs and how they influence their moods and behaviors. CBT trains you to notice when your thinking is distorted so that you can eventually stand back and question its validity.

Say you're meeting a guy for a blind date and he doesn't show up. You may think this means he's found out who you are and as a result finds you so hideous, he's ditched out. Cognitive therapy would help you to rethink your reaction and introduce the possibility that you overreacted and that maybe he got the wrong address or just overslept. With CBT you learn to test the usefulness and meaning of various thoughts you have and to change the thinking patterns that hold you locked in dysfunctional behaviors, moods, and relationships. It may stop you from yelling, when you do meet up with the no-show date, "I know that you're disgusted by me but I find you repulsive too." You will have lost your dignity and he will have no idea what you're talking about.

CBT can be used for low self-confidence, guilt, stress, depression, apathy, the breakup of relationships, pressure at school, phobias, and the inability to move on from the fact you lost the egg and spoon race at age eight. Any time, in fact, where you're stuck in habitual thinking, feeling, or behaving. The theory is that your thoughts, moods, behaviors, and physical reaction are all interconnected in that they affect each other like falling dominos; your thinking affects your moods, which affect your behavior, and vice versa. If you change how you think, it affects how you physically feel, which changes how you behave, which changes your mood.

> *Negativity is nearly always based on distortions of thinking.*

CBT also illustrates the fact that negativity is nearly always based on distortions of thinking; it's what makes you feel worthless, dumb, helpless, and so on. A depressed mind filters out anything that contradicts the negative onslaught. Fewer phone calls or finding out about a party you haven't been invited to could trigger feelings of rejection that might drive you to hide in your bed for a week (thanks, Facebook). You will remain lost unless you do something about it, such as changing your thinking. All of us have our own homemade package of distorted thinking ready to bring out whenever we feel threatened or stressed.

Examples of Distorted Thinking

- **All or nothing thinking.** When you evaluate a situation you see it as either black or white; no gray in sight, even though we all know there are fifty-seven shades or whatever there are.

- **Overgeneralization.** Here you randomly come to the conclusion that if something happens to you it will happen again and again. You will notice if you're suffering from this syndrome because your sentences will start with, "This always happens . . . ," "This is typical . . . ," "Every time I do that it happens . . . ," "This stuff happens only to me . . ." Sound familiar? Welcome to overgeneralization (my world).

- **Mental filter.** You see everything in the world as not being even as a glass half empty but as a glass completely broken into a million pieces on the floor and you'll probably cut your foot on one of the shards.

- **Disqualifying the positive.** A magical trick where, before your very eyes, you can transform a positive experience, hey presto, into a negative one. This is where any compliment is seen as a fiction invented for ulterior motives. When I got into Oxford, I assumed it was because they were just after my money for the enrolment fees (this still might actually be true). When I was in a mental institution for my depression, I assumed the staff members were being nice only because of the massive fees I was paying and that they really hated me.

- **Jumping to conclusions.** Also called mind reading. If I look out at an audience and notice one person with their head down or eyes not pointing at me, I know immediately I have flopped and probably will flop for the rest of my life.

- **Magnification and minimization.** This is another favorite of mine. It occurs when you either blow things up or shrink them down, depending on whichever one is more hurtful. So you awfulize your failures and hardly mention the award you won.

- **Emotional reasoning.** This is the one where you think that your emotions are telling you the truth. So because you often say you're stupid, you must therefore have something wrong in your brain. My mother used to tell me she thought something was wrong with my brain because she imagined some chemical was released just before she escaped from Austria. (I do not know what chemical she was referring to but she stood by her beliefs.)

- **Should/ought/must statements.** These are very popular for everyone. The inner voice thinks it's helping by adding, "I must have . . . [fill in anything]" to supplement your supply of self-loathing. Some people call it "musturbation."

- **Labeling and mislabeling.** This is when you smack a label on yourself and believe it. If you win a silver medal in the four hundred meters at the Olympics and then call yourself a loser, you might be mislabeling.

- **Personalization.** You imagine everything is your fault even when you had nothing to do with it. There's an earthquake; it has nothing to do with your bad moods. My phone used to break constantly. I believed it picked up my anger and hormonal rage and that the crackle of my vibes killed it.

Doing CBT—The Homework

Your CBT therapist will give you homework each week and encourage you to record your reactions and note down alternative responses to particular situations that push your buttons. The recording of your thoughts, moods, and physical feelings gives you distance, which allows you to have objectivity when you're testing their validity. There are myriad different CBT exercises. Here is just one example:

The Situation
Who?
What?
When?
Where?

Moods
Depressed
Sad

Ashamed

Guilty

Frightened

Panicky

Happy

Hurt

Scared

Nervous

Humiliated

I'm sure you have your own theme song.

Rating Moods

After you identify each mood you experience, you rate its intensity, and by doing this you begin to notice how your moods fluctuate.

Rate from 0 to 100

0 = No feeling at all

100 = The most you've ever felt

Automatic Thoughts

What was going through your mind just before you started to feel this way? Any other thoughts? Images? By using this exercise, you may start to notice themes, and these are your automatic thoughts. For example:

Everyone hates me
I don't deserve this
I'm a failure
I'm going to get caught
I'm a loser
I'm being taken advantage of
People are lying to me

Physical Sensations
Nausea
Cramping
Butterflies
Gassy (not good in meetings)
Pounding in the heart
Shakiness
Weakness
Dizziness
Numbness
Tingling
Vomiting (also not good in meetings)

Alternative/Balanced Thoughts
Is there an alternative way of thinking about the situation?
If you were with a friend who asked for advice because this
was happening to her, how would you help her deal with the
situation?

Action Plans

These are plans to help you solve the problems that you've identified. Write as many helpful suggestions as you can think of to move forward in the eventuality of a similar situation. Write as if you were advising a friend.

Rate Moods Now

After filling in the CBT Spreadsheet, rate the moods listed in the Moods column as well as any new moods on a scale from 0 to 100, based on intensity.

EXAMPLE OF CBT SPREADSHEET: FILL IN YOUR OWN

SITUATION	MOODS	RATING MOODS 0-100	AUTOMATIC THOUGHTS
Who? What? When? Where?	Examples: Sad Hurt Anxious		Examples: I'm a failure No one likes me I should have ...

EXAMPLE OF CBT SPREADSHEET: FILL IN YOUR OWN

PHYSICAL SENSATIONS	ALTERNATIVE/ BALANCED THOUGHTS	ACTION PLANS	RATE MOODS NOW 0-100
Examples: Nausea Heart pounding	Examples: Don't sweat the small stuff. You did the best you could.	Examples: Next time get professional help. Take a holiday.	

My Personal CBT Spreadsheet

Situation

A while back, I found myself driving at top speed to get to an appointment on time for something so shallow I don't even want to mention it. The appointment for this shallow thing was at 11:00 a.m. I had arranged for a plumber to come over between 9:30 and 10:30 a.m. to fix my boiler. I would have to leave at the latest at 10:15 to make my appointment. He arrived at 10:10 (which is a miracle in itself), but I was now going to be late. He took a long time gazing at my boiler and then did what plumbers do best, told me an endless fairytale about how my cylinder was already out of date in the Dark Ages and I'd need a replacement. At 10:40, I decided I had to take a shower (based on insanity). In the rush, I forgot to open the shower door, banged into it and had a nosebleed. As I dressed quickly, I ripped my underwear trying to get both legs in one hole. At 10:50, I got into my car and drove down a one-way street, giving the finger to oncoming cars driving past me.

Just a note: I think I inherited this addiction to lateness and giving myself an adrenaline rush from my mother who used to hunt for dust balls under the sofa while my dad was honking the horn to drive her to the airport. Once she arrived in the UK with no luggage, only the dress on her back but dammit she got that dust ball before she left, and in the world of OCD that was all that mattered.

Moods and Rating of Intensity
Self-loathing 85
Panicked 95
Furious 92
Frustrated 75
Nervous 99

Automatic Thoughts

Mainly devil voices. "I'm a f— up, sh— cu— fu— ass— wipe— cu—. I'm getting my nails painted, my f—ing nails!" (That was what the appointment was for.) "I'm so ashamed, most of the rest of the world are dying and I'm having the tips of my fingers painted. And worse I'm going to drive over people and kill them to have it done."

Physical Sensations

Sweat dripping off my face and neck. Hard and quick breathing, then no breathing at all. Heart like a drum solo at a heavy metal concert. Forehead held in vise grip.

Alternative/Balanced Thoughts

- Screaming will not make you move any faster.
- Take off your watch and hide it. Looking at your watch continuously won't make you move any faster.
- At a stoplight think to yourself that it's far better to stay alive than to have blue nails. You can have blue nails when you're dead.
- Try to bring some awareness to your body and send relaxation to areas you notice might be a little tight.

    Uncurl your toes.

    Unwrench your neck.

    Unhump your shoulders.

    Unclench your jaw.

    Smile.

- Do not get angry with yourself for this highly pressured incident. Just say, "I'm going to plan better next time" and give yourself a little hug. (A little irony went on there if you remember my views on hugging—not great.)

Action Plans

Next time you arrange it, make the appointment with the plumber at another time, another day, or another year but not minutes before you need to go somewhere. Get yourself a lovely calendar with lilies on it and write down your appointments. When you have completed them, give yourself a gold star next to the date.

Put an X with tape on your shower door so you don't bang into it again.

Maybe think about how unnecessary it is to paint your nails blue in the big scheme of things.

Intensity of Moods Now

About 25 percent. (Ta-da!)

Do not, I repeat, do not, punish yourself for being late or say to yourself, "I screwed up again" or "It's my parents' fault." You have probably been someone who's late for a long time. If you try to figure out why, bring out the welcome mat to rumination.

MY STORY

Another example of my anxiety triggers: I have invited guests for dinner, and it's now one hour before they arrive. I'm frantically fingering through my stain-covered collection of cookbooks that I never use. The words mean nothing to me and the photos are too intimidating, reminding me of my inability to do anything domestic. If I actually tuned in to what I'm thinking it would be total contempt for the people I've invited over. The minute they said yes to my invitation, I resented them for making me go through this. I know that I invited them, but I hate them now, and I hate myself for inviting them.

Half an hour before the guests arrive, I decide to call people who can cook to help me. (Once I even called Nigella, who thought I was joking and hung up.) I have now started to call random people in my contacts, offering any amount of cash if they will come over and cook dinner for the twelve friends I will never speak to again. When that fails, I will get in my car, in full hunting mode and drive up and down the street, looking frantically out of the window as if someone were going to come up to me with a tray full of ready-cooked meals.

Ten minutes before guest time, I have found myself running up and down the aisles of a supermarket not knowing what goes with what and then hurling myself before a butcher begging for him to tell me how and what to stuff a lamb chop with because these are fancy people coming over. You can't just throw them a plain lamb chop, it has to be something stuffed; this makes me hate them even more. As the butcher explains, I have no idea what he's talking about but write it down with shaking hands. I'm still trying to call Nigella on my mobile but she's not answering.

I drive home swerving to avoid killing off whole families, then run into the kitchen turning on the oven, realizing it doesn't heat up right away so I do what I always do—scream at the oven to hurry up—and then the doorbell rings. I shriek through the intercom, "Come in, just a minute," then run upstairs tripping several times, tearing off my clothes and take that crucial shower I always take when I'm really in a hurry. I slide out, smashing into the same shower door, wipe some eye shadow near my eye, grab any clothes, fall down the stairs, and open the door, trying to sound casual while noticing I'm wearing something crumpled I just took out of the laundry basket.

Then I realize with complete horror that I've forgotten to buy any finger foods for them to nibble on (God I hate that word). I skip backward into the kitchen opening the cabinets so hard one of the doors falls off and find some old ham and peanut butter and (luckily) toothpicks. I begin to rip the ham into squares, stick the toothpicks in and smear just a little peanut butter on top. I open my fridge and to my delight find an olive and add it to the ham/peanut butter hors d'oeuvres.

The rest of the evening is a travesty because I've thrown wine back into my mouth so fast, I do a monologue without noticing no one is laughing or even listening. After an hour or two I'm still going, telling stories repeatedly with no punchline. Doing a CBT spreadsheet might have been very useful.

My Wedding

I couldn't find the ring that Ed bought me, and it was the morning of my wedding. We were going to be married in a registry office because I had been married twice before: once to a gay person, to get a permit for me to work in the UK, and another time to get a permit for another gay person to help him work in America. The magic of a white wedding, needless to say, had been sucked out of me.

With hardly any notice, I invited everyone the day before and when I got to the registry office (late), as we walked toward the registrar, I whispered to Ed how old I really was and that I'd been married twice before—had he known before the event he might have tried to bolt. Due to my lateness, I couldn't find the wedding ring so I just grabbed the receipt, and wrapped it around my finger for all to see and admire the actual price. It was a travesty.

Not Everyone Is Late

There are people in the world—I've heard rumors, it may be true—who actually appear at events and appointments early, but I cannot relate to them so I won't write about them. Perhaps being early could be another type of distorted thinking. The action is propelled by another kind of nagging voice, "I can't be late. If I'm late no one will respect/like/love me." Whichever way you go, late or early, it definitely disturbs your well-being.

My Quibble with CBT

CBT works for so many people, I don't want to throw a wrench in the works but I thought I'd throw in my opinion, which is always a wrench. If you're continually digging up thoughts and feelings even though you're standing back and noting them down, they might spark off self-critical and repetitive, negative thinking, which are forerunners of an assault of depression.

Words are what keep you captive in your head so remembering and documenting perpetuates the voices. To put everything into words means the mind has to travel to the past, thereby strengthening past and future thinking, pulling you out of experiencing the present.

Evidence of How Mindfulness Produces Better Results Than CBT

John Teasdale, who helped develop MBCT, tested the efficacy of mindfulness compared with CBT on a group of clinically depressed patients in remission. He found that the relapse rate into another depressive episode differed dramatically. About 62 percent of patients given traditional CBT relapsed compared to 36 percent of those who did MBCT. The researchers measured metacognition and those who could achieve it were the ones least likely to relapse.

EXERCISE: SELF-REGULATION WITH THE TRAFFIC SIGNAL GAME

EMOTIONAL INTELLIGENCE

Self-regulation is beginning to be taught to kids at primary schools, alongside the academic syllabus. (About time.) Think of the advantages these kids will have over us. They learn before they send blame (or start to bully, or think the world is unfair) how their own emotions work, which for some strange reason has never been taught before or hardly mentioned, as far as I know.

TRAFFIC SIGNALS

When a child feels he is leaving his neutral (calm) zone and heading toward stress, fear, anxiety, sadness, or panic, he holds up a *red card*.

All other people are not allowed to come within a six-feet radius; they are told to just leave him alone.

When the child feels his stress levels coming down, he holds up a *yellow card*.

When he feels he is back to his baseline of calm he holds up a *green card*.

Now the teacher helps him process what went on for him. He learns to understand what he's bringing into the room instead of projecting it out onto other people, believing that they caused his feelings. He may well be reacting to others, but they did not cause his emotions; only he can create them and only he can reduce them. So he has learned to regulate his feelings.

Imagine how useful this would be in an office when a meeting gets emotionally hot. When people lose their neutral baseline of calm and the emotional temperatures get too high, the rest of the meeting is a waste of time and energy. When people *lock antlers* they get into a fight mode; the original argument goes out the window, and now it's just biological warfare. (Your biology.) The people involved virtually go *out of their minds*; their memory goes down because cortisol is now killing off neurons in the hippocampus; blood leaves the brain; breathing becomes shallow, stopping oxygenation in the brain; and now they're looking for a fight, not a solution.

How great it would be if as adults we could recognize when we're heading toward a meltdown, hold up the red card or even just a white flag of surrender that says, "Meeting over, I'm crazy right now. I'll be back when I'm normal." Imagine how many wars we could avoid if we knew we were aware that we're carrying the dynamite (our own emotions) and knew how to back off. If we could recognize that we might be the weapons of mass destruction ourselves all would be well in the world.

If we had a manual (which I've been going on about for a while), it would instruct you that if you're going to an interview, audition, business meeting, head-to-head with your friends or family in a highly charged state, back off and come back later; otherwise it will only end in tears.

EXERCISE: REDECORATING YOUR INSIDES

If you're feeling overwhelmed by stress, worry, anger, fear, write down at least three situations or moments you consider to be positive, however small. Emotions are as transient as pain; write down when you have a moment where you notice a feeling that might be, dare I say it, positive. Write down the situation when you felt this positive feeling, along with the date and time.

EXAMPLE

September 13, 4:04 p.m.—Someone smiled at me on the bus. Got a twinge of lightness and heart twang of happiness. (Don't write, "They probably thought I was someone else.")

November 11, 2:37 p.m.—My cat sat on my lap and I felt velvet in my chest.

December 24, 8:00 a.m.—I saw a red Christmas bauble and was pinged with pleasure. (No one will see your journal so don't be embarrassed by how schmaltzy you might sound.)

All of this is to build up a storage space of memories of feeling good that you can call up at will. When you become aware of these breaks in the weather, your brain is unwiring from the embedded negative patterns, and each time you're aware of a positive sensation the brain fires with new patterns. (Building more positive muscles.)

EXERCISE: SELF-REGULATION USING SMELL

I have a friend who told me there's a candle with a scent called winter that reminds her of Christmas when she was a child: part warm gingerbread cookies, part pine trees. She told me that whenever she smells it, she feels as if she were in the body of her ten-year-old self and a feeling of sweetness spreads throughout her body; she feels her shoulders melt down and her eyes go soft. Before a meeting or appointment that's unnerving, she brings out the candle and sniffs it when no one's looking and the soothing feeling returns. She goes into the meeting in this open and relaxed state, able to take the bumps; her mind calm so she can think clearly, creatively, and quickly. If she suddenly gets a spike of anxiety she excuses herself, goes to the ladies' room, and sits there smelling the candle, bringing herself back to neutral. This is self-regulating at its best—knowing how to manage your inner state and doing something about it.

EXERCISE: SELF-REGULATION USING SIGHT

My friend Joanna carries a photo of herself in midair on a zip line. Whenever she brings it out to look at it, she's back up there, flying through the trees. When she knows she has to face some challenging event, she peeks at the picture. I once watched her give a speech on stage. I could tell when her confidence started to ebb because she'd glance at the lectern where I knew she had the photo. Each time she looked at it her whole body relaxed, her voice got stronger, her eyes relaxed and she got back her sense of humor. (That's the first thing to sink when you lose your nerve.) She told me that as soon as she senses a small stab of fear just knowing the photo is nearby gets her right back to that sense of freedom, flying in the trees.

This could be a useful tool in business for presentations. I have watched heads of big organizations stand on stage giving their PowerPoint presentations with those graphs of success going up and down, meaning nothing to anyone. They may have the brains to be the CEO but they have no idea that they have put the whole audience into a coma, droning on and on about values or profits or who cares what—no one's listening. If the speaker is disconnected from what he's saying, and from the moment, everyone else will be too. Snapping back into the present, the dullard at the podium could try to change course—crack a joke or mention that people aren't really responding and ask for suggestions. Any of these alternatives to the coma-inducing state can win back an audience.

ALTERNATIVES

You can also prime your positive emotions with:

- **Sound.** Listen to a piece of music before a stressful event (whatever rocks your boat). I have a recording of sounds from the jungle, parrots squawking and rain dripping. As soon as I listen to it, I'm on holiday, and my body goes calm. I don't care who's shouting at me in those moments.
- **Touch.** Grab a swatch of cashmere that you like to touch (or leather for those of you who might be into that) to bring you back to normal (whatever it means).
- **Taste.** Feeling tense? Put a sweet in your mouth. (Choose something small or you'll just be chewing in someone's face forever, which will actually worsen the stress).

IN THE BRAIN

Using any one of sense-provoking stimuli can promote feelings of well-being, which has physiological repercussions: You feel good, so you get an increase in dopamine to get that motivated feeling. (Just enough makes you feel positive and keen to accomplish things; too much and you're chasing your tail.)

When you intentionally use an image that calms you down, you're immediately lowering the amygdala and re-routing activity to your prefrontal cortex, which promotes higher thinking and better decision making. When you're in this positive state, you're increasing neural growth, enhancing learning and more workspace in the memory.

Also, when you focus on something that brings out a positive reaction—your child's face or your cat curled up in a salad bowl (mine does that, it's adorable)—brain scanning shows that the areas that are responsible for calming you down become more activated. Whether you see something in actuality or picture it in your mind, the same area lights up in the brain. If you touch something warm, the same area in your brain lights up as when you feel emotional warmth. So simply by using images of things that make you feel good, you're activating the "feel good" area. This is really *using your brain*.

EXERCISE: OPENING YOUR LENS WITH NOVELTY

Using a journal, write down when you notice something you've seen for the first time. Start with three entries a day. For example:

> My daughter has yellow in her green eyes.
> That tree has buds on it.
> I can hear a clock ticking from the next room.
> My dog's bark is different from that of my neighbor's dog.
> This blade of grass is greener than the other one.

Reminder: Novelty grows neurons.

EXERCISE: YOUR GRATITUDE

I used to make fun of my friend Kathy, who told me she writes down a few things each day she's grateful for. I could never imagine doing that because I find it a bit frilly, but she seems much calmer and happier these days, so who am I to say? She tells me that no matter how dark things get she will find that gap of light. For example:

> I have two legs.
> I can taste ice cream.
> I am alive.

EXERCISE: LABELING

My friend Tanya told me that as soon as she recognizes one of her critical voices that's giving her hell, she labels it. This gives her distance from the onslaught.

She told me she was called back to a job interview four times, and after the fourth was rejected. Rather than think, "Well, I got close that time, I'll get a job at some point soon" (I have yet to meet someone who thinks like that), her habitual stab-in-her-own-back response was "I'm never going to get a job." She told me as soon as she hears her familiar theme, she labels it as "Worrying."

When she starts to berate herself for failing, she labels it "Berating."

When she panics that she's never going to get a job, she labels it "Panicking."

When she starts creating scenarios where she's homeless and Prada-less, she labels it as "Fantasizing" or "Catastrophizing." I would also call it "Pradasizing."

The labeling identifies and defuses the hot emotions and negative thoughts. If thoughts and feelings have labels, they are no longer some solid part of you but transient items that come and go. It's as if you were saying, "Oh, that's anxiety" (out there) rather than "I am anxious" (in me).

EXERCISE: NAMING THE DEMON

Whenever I used to get a sniff of rejection, I would slide straight back to the feeling I had as a child: lonely, ignored, and a little freakish. The incident could be as minuscule as not being invited to a birthday party. I'd immediately jump to the conclusion that they had found out I was a freak from my childhood records.

Whenever I got that feeling, I gave it a name: Mitzi. I'd think, "OK, I'm now in the Mitzi mode." I had a very distinct picture in my mind of her: ratty hair, a dirty face, scrawny, and wearing rags. (Not dissimilar to a character in *Oliver* but with an American accent.) Whenever I'd feel that black hole of despair and rejection, I'd bring up the image of Mitzi, which in turn made me feel compassion for her (myself). I realized this is an eccentric way of dealing with depression. (I would go and write this up in a book and get it published but it turns out I am doing that.)

DEALING WITH MY OTHER DEMONS

Besides Mitzi, I gave my other demons a name too.

STELLA

When I get a bit of envy I picture Stella. She's blond, wears a floaty white toga, and has pointy teeth with blood on them. Stella pulls the pain right out of me and I can watch her objectively. She cries a lot so I sit her on my lap and console her and the agony passes.

FRED

When I used to get a whiff of anger, I would feel myself transform from a woman to a werewolf. I have a trigger finger when it comes to rage. In the past I'd even seek out situations where I could provoke people so I could vent my reptilian anger on them. I would hunt down innocent people (never friends). I'd find a snappy bus driver, a librarian who told me my book was overdue and tear into them until they were just a pile of bones. The fury was addictive and tasted delicious while I was in mid-spew; the problem was that hours later I'd suffer something like a serious hangover from all the poison I'd thrown about.

It all comes back to you. That is the lesson I learned. I had to start to muzzle the beast and by giving it this image, I'd just watch it bark and snarl and spit until it was exhausted and then slink away whimpering.

EXERCISE: HABIT BREAKERS

Each tiny change of habit you make opens up a small chink in the wall you've built around yourself; keep on changing, and you'll be able to break free from the prison you've created. *Small steps make big changes.*

The chair you're used to sitting on—change it.
The route you drive/walk/take a train to work—change it.

The type of people you like to be around—mix it up a bit.

Sleep on the other side of the bed.

Change to another brand of toothpaste/perfume/lipstick/
soup.

(Maybe think twice before you change your husband/
wife.)

EXERCISE: FAKING IT TO MAKE IT

It seems that your facial expressions can change how you feel.
In one experiment, researchers asked students to hold a pencil between their teeth in order to give them the physical
appearance of smiling. They were then asked to rate their
feelings while looking at neutral photos. The ones with the
pencils said the photos made them feel good while those not
smiling (pencil-less) said they made them feel either nothing
or sad. Not only did the experiment evoke positive feelings

in the person with the pencil, it created positive feelings in other people (mainly because they laughed at the people with the pencil in their mouths).

Don't laugh; just smile and put a pencil in your mouth.

EXERCISE: TOTAL DISTRACTION

. . . .

If emotions or thoughts get too hot, be good to yourself and totally switch your attention to take down the heat. (Try not to pick something that will harm you, such as drugs, too much food, or overshopping.)

Start counting backward from 100 to 1.
Watch television/a film.
Listen to loud music.
Read something shallow or this book.
Run/walk/dance/swim . . .

EXERCISE: ATTENTIVE LISTENING AND TALKING (RAPPORT)

. . . .

To be done in pairs.

STEP ONE
. . . .

For one minute, talk to each other.

Now turn your backs to each other and each person describe what color eyes the other one has, what her hair is like (color), and what the other is wearing. This helps us realize how little we notice what's right in front of our eyes.

STEP TWO

. . . .

Try again—take it in turns for each of you to talk to each other for another minute.

If you're the listener, notice:

What her body language is saying
Her tone of voice
What words she chooses
What she might mean under the words

If you're the talker, notice:

How the other person is reacting to what you're saying
What emotions you're reading
When the other person looks like she wants to say something

STEP THREE

. . . .

Now both discuss what you were thinking and feeling; were there any inner voices? This is the best way to instantly bond with someone else.

COMPASSION AND KINDNESS

A human being experiences himself, his thoughts and feelings, as something separated from the rest. . . . This delusion is a kind of prison for us. . . . Our task must be to free ourselves from this prison by widening our circles of compassion to embrace all living creatures and the whole of nature in its beauty.

—ALBERT EINSTEIN

. . .

The essence of neuroplasticity is that what you practice you'll cultivate. If you are cruel and spiteful, you'll become expert at getting even more cruel and spiteful. If you practice being compassionate, you'll become more compassionate. That's how our brains work; the way we think or feel determines our wiring and what chemicals are coursing through our veins. If you're thinking or feeling agitated or angry you're pumping adrenaline and cortisol. If you're feeling love or compassion you've got some of that good old oxytocin fueling you. Again, we limit ourselves by believing we're born a certain way and we'll always remain that way.

To change the brain, all you need to do is put effort in it. For some of us, feeling positive is very challenging. I know how to do hurt, but being nice has not been part of my repertoire. If having a feeling of kindness or compassion is vague, you need to familiarize yourself with how it feels in your body and mind. Over time and with practice you may go from a twinge to a full feeling. The goal is still to experience feelings, even positive ones, as transitory; they all pass so you're not aiming at holding on to a feeling of beatific bliss but of equanimity, of going with the flow.

I don't want to steal ideas from Alcoholics Anonymous, which says "Accept the things you cannot change and change the things you can," but I couldn't say it any better.

The opposite of self-criticism is self-compassion, and this can be cultivated. For example, bring to mind something that moves you—for example, a bunny rabbit (no one will find out) or your baby. Notice how kindness and affection feel in your body. The feelings of kindness are an antidote for when you feel sad or depressed. If you're in that kindness state, watch how your words and actions affect what you're doing or who you're talking to. These feelings spread out and when you feel good, others catch it and send it right back to you.

It's not so hard to send kindness to things and people you love. The more advanced course is when you deliberately send it to someone who has upset you or you don't like. If you can, the results are always positive, and if you can't, just forgive yourself because letting yourself off the hook is also kindness.

A Story . . .

One evening, a Native American elder told his grandson about a battle that goes on inside people. He said, "My son, the battle is between two wolves inside us all. One is anger, envy, jealousy, sorrow, regret, greed, arrogance, self-pity, guilt, resentment, inferiority, lies, false pride, and superiority. The other is joy, peace, love, hope, serenity, humility, kindness, benevolence, empathy, generosity, truth, and compassion." The grandson thought about it for a minute and then asked his grandfather, "Which wolf wins?" The elder simply replied, "The one that you feed."

EXERCISE: MINDFULNESS IN MOTION

. . . .

Everyone knows that physical exercise improves your health, longevity, physical and mental state, and generally makes you feel better about yourself. A hit of your own endorphins is almost better than any drug you can buy over or under the counter. My only problem with the blanket expression *get some exercise* is that most of us do it without thinking; we just jerk our bodies around, squat, push, kick, or scrunch in the hope of harder pecs. You see people in the gym, running on the treadmill for hours, reading a book, watching the news, their minds millions of miles away from what their feet are doing. This could be called mindless exercise, which in the end does more damage than good. I've watched people do a thousand sit-ups in under two minutes, knowing that they will very shortly pull every disc they've got. When I came to England in the 1970s, no one was even brushing their teeth; now they have to go to the gym every day before and after work. Men of all ages suddenly need a six-pack. For what? In case they suddenly get cast to go topless in an aftershave ad? Suddenly everywhere there are these amphitheaters with hundreds of male and female bums grinding away to MTV; rock solid babes, their leotards lodged somewhere in their liver they're cut so high. On the running machines you see elderly people, hunched over, nearly dead but their little stick legs are moving just because the treadmill is still switched on; if they stop they'll be sucked under the belt never to be seen again, just a pair of false teeth left behind.

Many people use exercise to try to attempt to run away from their uncomfortable emotions or thoughts. Out they jump at 5:00 a.m. and do whatever they have to do to cut themselves off from their voices. The voices will eventually win out because when you can no longer run, pole vault, or even walk (and I don't want to depress you but this will happen) your mind will still be in the state you left it. The bottom line is that *you have to exercise your brain as much as you do your body.*

Dance, jump, hump, flip, high-kick all you want when you're young, you're made to be bouncy, but at a certain point, mindless exercise isn't good for you, and you may rip something and hurt yourself very badly.

The idea is to be able to exercise the part of your body you want to exercise while everywhere else is relaxed—this is how you get toned, not tensed. Again, this is using intentional attention. A fit muscle is one that's strong but released, not stiff and contracted and you can only have that if you attend to the area you're working out.

These days, professional athletes are trained to sit still with their eyes closed and imagine the movements their muscles need to make when they're actually competing. Besides the physical training, they are virtually picturing their grip on the tennis racket, their arm lifting, the other arm throwing up the ball, slamming it down, and so on, and as they imagine these moves, neuronal connections are wiring together in the equivalent area of the motor cortex. When it comes to the actual play, they have primed the correct muscles so they'll be able to move faster and play harder in the real game. It's the mental training of attention, not pure physical training, that increases memory and learning capabilities.

The best exercise is done when you're sensing what you're moving, flexing, lifting, pushing, and pumping. Some examples of mindful practices are Pilates, yoga, tai chi, qigong, and martial arts.

All of these can be done mindlessly too, but part of the training is to make sure every move is sensed from the inside. Breath is used to connect the body and the mind, and each move is closely observed moment by moment. These practices are, in my opinion, mindfulness in movement: sharpening attention and focus and bringing you to a state of calm and peace. On the other hand, when I do Zumba (I think I'm fantastic at this until I look in the mirror), I just let myself go with the flow, not really thinking about my breath or what my body is doing. It's all about consciously choosing when you want automatic pilot and when you don't.

CURIOSITY

Curiosity is what makes us superior to dust mites. Sadly, many people don't use it. They have it, but it has become obsolete. We are born with this feature. That's why when we're children, our hunger for information is insatiable; we don't even care what the story is, we just want to be stimulated. That is how our brains grow and how, as more and more neurons connect, we become smarter. Then comes school. The point of going is, we hope, to ignite that nascent curiosity in more ways—history, math, religion, literature, and so on. Millions of years ago they didn't have school, but it was a matter of life and death for the kids to learn how to make a fire, beat animals senseless with rocks, and wash their hands before they went to the loo.

These days, I feel that what kills the spark of curiosity is the fact that everything hangs on a grade. Nothing will burn out an interest quicker. I'm aware that high grades get you into a great university where you will go to the best parties, but if you get hooked on this chasing the grade thing and (even worse) if your parents push you too hard, you might find that you get the habit of chasing a rabbit for the rest of your life, thinking that there will be some reward in front of you, always just out of reach. And when you conquer something, it might not be for the personal satisfaction of attaining a goal but rather for beating the competition.

So curiosity goes out the window and competitive spirit steps in. Again, you need it and it's not a bad trait, but when you end up studying law when your passion is pottery, it's a sad state of affairs. True, we don't need so many wheel-thrown pots and it's hard to sell them but at least you might experience satisfaction in your life, even though you'll probably need to be on welfare. If you do things simply for gaining more cash, fame, status, power, or an A+, misery or madness lie in your path.

My final word on this is that only if you find something you love doing, and then do it, is life worth living. (I tell that to my daughters adding that they should marry someone rich who'll be able to afford the pursuit of their dreams.) To me, the most important and beneficial of all exercises is the strengthening of your curiosity, because that is the glue that binds the human race. If you are curious about someone else, and show it, it is the most flattering thing you can do for them; they will give you anything—the keys to their car, their business, they'll probably even marry you. I have a friend who decides in minutes if she wants to go on a date with someone by timing how long it takes him to say *you* rather than *I*. Most people don't ask questions, and some of the most brilliant people I know (with IQs off the planet) have no curiosity and are therefore idiots.

If we practice how to attend to one another and not just win debates or show each other how much information we can stuff in our heads, we would evolve a truly civilized world. In business, if you learn to listen and be curious about another person and pay attention to how he feels, negotiations would be a breeze. Huge amounts of money, time, and energy are wasted by people talking at each other rather than with each other. There should be training simply to learn how to be curious rather than endless MBA programs. People are what sells, nothing else. You like and trust the person, you'll do business with them and if you are genuinely curious, people won't be able to resist you. If you learn to speak and listen mindfully, stepping out of your habitual patterns of behavior, you will reduce interpersonal conflicts, stereotyping, and cross-cultural misunderstanding.

FINAL NOTE

The main message of mindfulness and of the exercises I presented in Part 5, is that change is all that we can be sure of, and our lives are uncertain. Holding on to anything only creates more suffering.

Everything changes all the time, from the volatility of quantum particles to every cell in our nervous system. Even our consciousness, probably located in our prefrontal cortex, is updated five to eight times a second. Thoughts come and go like each breath we take; they come, disperse and disappear.

Life is much more than scratching the itch of wanting something and chasing the dragon. (See Jimmy Choo shoes.) With practice, we can learn to recognize when our minds have taken us hostage to somewhere in the past or future, and then focus on what's really out there (sound, taste, touch, sight, smell, or the breathing). The only thing keeping us from being present is our thoughts, and thoughts aren't facts.

In order to survive, your brain fools you into making you believe that there are fixed patterns in this chaotic world and that we can actually create permanent plans. Our brains are constantly chasing after a moment that has just passed, trying to control it. It's like taking a photo of a waterfall and believing it's actually stopped in time. Everything is gone before you even register it. It is now . . . and now it's gone and so in a sense everything is memory.

When you were a kid, those neurons were firing every second; everything was novel and exciting, you'd say things like, "I want to be a fireman or an astronaut," with absolutely no consideration of qualifications required. (I wanted to be a mermaid.) Everything is possible—you can look at a snowflake for hours and configure cloud clusters as neighborhoods. "That cloud is my house and that one is my bedroom and I can jump to your cloud and visit and have tea." Everything was fresh back then, in full living Technicolor, and you were excited out of your mind. You get older some asshole tells you, you can't be a mermaid, for whatever reason, or you can't fly like Superman. As you get older, your world gets tinier and tinier because you believe you don't have options until you die in a rut.

And no one seems to care that we end up growing into such a tiny part of our potential; we just think, "Oh well, this is how I ended up." We say about old people, "Oh, that's just Grandma" or "Boo Poo," or "Kree Kree," or whatever we're calling them now (when you're old you're treated like a pet). "Oh, that's just Granny. She does the same thing every day—she has her tea at four, then walks her dog at five, naps at six, and then beddy byes."

This is how and why our brains atrophy, because we start to say the same thing over and over again without anyone telling you, "Shut up, you said that before." When you're old you don't want to change chairs, countries, learn the tango, parachute jump (you're old—what's the worst that could happen?). Improvise your life, grow some new neurons. That's how everything becomes fresh again, and you could even end up a mermaid.

And if you allow your thoughts to drive you, and you believe that your reality is the same as everyone else's, you'll become hard, judgmental, and intolerant and it will choke you in the end with bitterness. The lens through which you see yourself and your world will become more and more narrow, until it's dull and you're dull and your world is dull. But you need to realize that we are constantly in flux, and everything changes constantly, even you. You're always in a state of "becoming." There is no point in grabbing on to anything—people, money, clothes, stuff. There is no safety anywhere because everything is the unknown.

And it does not matter how much you have to let go of. If you only end up with the gift of simply noticing things as if for the first time, notice their novelty, it will outweigh how much stuff you've accumulated or what job you ended up with. The idea is to be able to let go so much that in the end you can say to your body, thanks for the ride and still be smiling (without a pencil in your mouth).

It's our ability to regulate our attention, reduce our reactive nature, and cultivate positive emotions that points the way to health and happiness. If we can calmly observe our own habits of thinking clearly, we can see it in others and have greater empathy. Increasing the limited view of how we see our world and ourselves should be the next phase of human evolution; to extend the breadth of our consciousness and expand our range of choices. This will lead to appropriate alternatives, and we'll be able to select each choice before we act on it. People who comprehend biological processes and make thoughtful choices shift from their self-centered world view to a much larger interconnected whole.

They can become wise people, make choices, and take actions that have long-term benefits for the future. The application of mindfulness will have an impact on social inequities, climate crisis, poverty, and disease. I hope, if nothing else, we move to a world where it's not survival of the fittest but survival of the wisest.

ACKNOWLEDGMENTS

I thank and kiss the ground before my friend and brilliant editor, Joanna Bowen. Without her, this book would be an incomprehensible jumble of random and unfathomable thoughts and oddly spelled words. She put chaos into order.

My professor of MBCT at Oxford University, Mark Williams, for being such an inspiration and passing his wisdom along with Melanie Fennell and John Peacock.

Dr. Mark Collins who saved me when I was deep in the darkness, and Ros who always holds my hand when I'm down there.

Rowena Webb, my publisher at Hodder and Stoughton, along with Maddy Price.

Thanks to Serge Seidlitz for his great illustrations.

To Michael Foster for setting all this up and my agent, Robert Caskie, along with Caroline Michel.

Andrew Dellis for his help with neuroscience. Simon Whitesman for his help with mindfulness.

My family, Ed, Maddy, Max, and Marina, for their constant supply of humor and endless supply of love.

My friends who stand by me. My parents who made me.

My relatives in America (the Hambourgers) who got my parents out of Austria just in time, without which I would not be possible.